Prayer
Bringing
Heaven to Earth

By A.L. and Joyce Gill

ISBN 0-941975-41-X

Copyright 1997
It is illegal and a violation of Christian ethics
to reproduce any part of this manual
without the written permission of the authors

Powerhouse Publishing
PO Box 99
Fawnskin, CA 92333
909-866-3119

Books by A.L. and Joyce Gill

God's Promises for Your Every Need

Destined for Dominion

Out! In the Name of Jesus

Victory over Deception

Manuals in This Series

Authority of the Believer
*How to Quit Losing
and Start Winning*

Church Triumphant
Through the Book of Acts

God's Provision for Healing
*Receiving and Ministering
God's Healing Power*

The Ministry Gifts
*Apostle, Prophet, Evangelist,
Pastor, Teacher*

Miracle Evangelism
God's Plan to Reach the World

New Creation Image
Knowing Who You Are in Christ

Patterns for Living
From the Old Testament

Praise and Worship
Becoming Worshipers of God

Supernatural Living
Through the Gifts of the Holy Spirit

Study Guides

Breakthrough to Glory

Set Free from Iniquity

Introduction

Prayer is an awesome privilege and absolute necessity to the successful Christian walk! And yet, as we talk to different people, listen to teaching tapes, or read book after book, it seems each one has a different understanding – even different definitions. To one, prayer is intercession. To another, it is warfare. To a third, it is talking to God and listening to Him. Prayer is all of these, and yet it's so much more.

Every truth in the Bible is built on another truth – it takes the whole to be complete. David wrote, The entirety of Your word is truth (Psalms 119:160). The apostle Paul wrote, I have not shunned to declare to you the whole counsel of God (Acts 20:27). However, our method of learning is still in bits and pieces.

We have never struggled with this reality more than in this study. Each lesson is a piece of the whole. We cannot study just one part and have an understanding of what true prayer is. Prayer is not just intercession. Prayer is not just listening to God. Prayer is not just speaking God's will forth. Prayer is not just asking. It's all of these.

We cannot base our lives or doctrines on the truths we like and ignore the rest. For example, we are the children of God and Jesus said that if we asked, we would receive. However, Jesus also said that if we are in sin, God cannot hear our prayers. One truth has direct correlation to the other. In a study on prayer, we cannot look only at the blessings. We must also look at the requirements that are made of us, and the responsibilities. We must study, to the best of our abilities, the whole counsel of God.

Year after year, we have hesitated to put this study together because there was, and is, always so much more to learn. We have been working through pages of notes written over a period of many years, and yet we know this can only be an introduction to prayer – an overall view. Whole books have been written on great truths of prayer that due to lack of space, we have covered in one or two paragraphs. Our prayer is that God will lead you through this study and then on into a lifetime of studying and experiencing prayer.

We have been asked why we include the scriptures in our text – there would be so much more we could say if we used only the references. After questioning hundreds of Bible students over the years, we have found very few who could say they looked up the references given in books as they were studying. We are aware that it's not our words, nor the words of any author, that are alive. Our words can only be an introduction to what He has said, a "pulling together" from the entirety of the Bible. God has promised us that His Word will not return void, that He is alert, actively watching over His Word to perform it. It is His words that are a joy and rejoicing in our hearts. Therefore, we have tried at all times to emphasize His Word.

So shall My word be that goes forth from My mouth; it shall not return to Me void,
but it shall accomplish what I please, and it shall prosper in the thing for which I sent it.
(Isaiah 55:11)

God is alert and active, watching over His Word to perform it.
(Jeremiah 1:12 Amp)

Your words were found, and I ate them,
and Your word was to me the joy and rejoicing of my heart.
(Jeremiah 15:16)

About the Authors

A.L. and Joyce Gill are internationally known speakers, authors and Bible teachers. A.L.'s apostolic ministry travels have taken him to over fifty nations of the world, preaching to crowds exceeding two hundred thousand in person and to many millions by radio and television.

Their top-selling books and manuals have sold over two million copies in the United States. Their writings, which have been translated into many languages, are being used in home groups, churches, Bible schools and seminars around the world.

The powerful life-changing truths of God's Word explode in the lives of others through their dynamic preaching, teaching, writing and tape ministry.

The awesome glory of the presence of God is experienced in their praise and worship seminars as believers discover how to become true and intimate worshipers of God. Many have discovered a new and exciting dimension of victory and boldness through their teachings on the authority of the believer.

The Gills have trained many believers to step into their own God-given supernatural ministries with the healing power of God flowing through their hands. Many have learned to be supernaturally natural as they are released to operate in all nine gifts of the Holy Spirit in their daily lives.

Both A.L. and Joyce have Master of Theological Studies degrees. A.L. also earned a Doctor of Philosophy in Theology degree from Vision Christian University. Their ministry is solidly based on the Word of God, is centered on Jesus, strong in faith and taught in the power of the Holy Spirit.

Their ministry is a demonstration of the Father's heart of love. Their preaching and teaching is accompanied by powerful anointing, signs, wonders, and healing miracles with many being slain in waves under the power of God.

Signs of revival including waves of holy laughter, weeping before the Lord and awesome manifestations of God's glory and power are being experienced by many who attend their meetings.

Table of Contents

Unless otherwise indicated all Scripture quotations
are taken from the New King James Version.
Copyright 1979, 1980, 1982, Thomas Nelson Inc., Publishers
The Amplified Bible *(Amp.) Copyright 1965 Zondervan Publishing House.*
The New International Bible *(NIV) Copyright 1973,1978,1984 International Bible Society.*
Use by permission of Zondervan Bible Publishers.

Suggested Reading

All the Prayers of the Bible
By Herbert Lockyer
Zondervan Publishing House

Art of Intercession
Kenneth Hagin
Harrison House

Effective Fervent Prayer
Mary Alice Isleib
Mary Alice Isleib Ministries

Intercessory Prayer
Dutch Sheets
Regal, A Division of Gospel Light

Life of Faith
Mrs. C. Nuzum
Radiant Books

Listening Prayer
Mary Ruth Swope
Whitaker House

**Possessing the Gates
Of the Enemy**
Cindy Jacobs
Chosen Books

Praying the Scriptures
Judson Cornwall
Creation House

**Shaping History
Through Prayer and Fasting**
Derik Prince – Fleming H. Revell

Lesson One

What is Prayer?

INTRODUCTION

Most Powerful Force

True prayer is the most powerful force in the world today. True prayer brings the force of our Almighty God into action. However, true prayer is sadly lacking in our generation.

Most Christians haven't been taught how to pray from the Word of God, but have learned by listening to or experiencing other, often erroneous examples.

In the church of our tradition, we had Wednesday night prayer meetings. We sat in a circle and everyone related their problems, and those of their family and friends. Then they told us what they thought the answer should be. When we bowed our heads to pray, our chief concern was that we had forgotten some of the problems and might not tell them to God. The next week, we heard the same problems and the same desire for answers. We talked about unruly teenagers until they grew up. We talked about Aunt Hilda's cancer until she died.

The Prayer Requests section in the church bulletin stayed almost the same week after week. We almost never heard of any answers to our prayers and after many years gave up going to prayer meetings. They were boring, negative times of dwelling only on the problems in everyone's life and nothing seemed to happen anyway.

Through this study, our goal is to take a new, fresh look at prayer. Through the numerous biblical examples, we will learn what prayer is and how to pray.

Rusty Nails

Years ago, we remodeled our kitchen. The first thing we had to do was tear out the old cabinets and counters, even some of the old walls, the ceiling and the floor. As wood ages, it gets very hard and some of the nails that needed to be pulled were three and four inches long. It took a large crowbar to remove them, and as some of them were pulled loose, they made a screeching sound – almost as if they were protesting.

Weeks after we had completed this project, during praise at the beginning of a service, I suddenly saw in the spirit one of these long rusty nails being pulled out. I heard the screech again. "Lord," I asked, "What is this?"

He said, "Those are the things you have been taught over the years that are in error. They are hard to remove, but they must be pulled out!"

Let's examine some of the "rusty nails" in our thinking about prayer.

Prayer Is Not

➪ **Begging a "reluctant" God to act on our behalf**

Many prayers sound like people are begging a reluctant God to act. They know God can act, but doubt His desire to do so for them because they are so unworthy.

➪ **Telling God our problems**

We hear people telling God their problems – as if He didn't already know them – and then we hear them telling God what they need Him to do. It's as if they give God a blueprint of what they want Him to do and then hope that He will do it.

If we pray continuously about the problems, they will grow larger and larger in our minds.

➪ **Convincing God of how worthy we are**

Many try to convince God of how worthy a person is. "God, Mary has always loved You. She has taught in the Sunday School for twenty years. She has been a good wife and mother. We need her, and we ask You to ..." That's basing prayer and faith on a person's goodness.

➪ **Persuading others of our relationship with God**

Some prayers seem as if they are prayed to persuade others of the great relationship the person has with God.

➪ **Expressions of doubt and unbelief**

Many of the prayers in the church of our tradition were expressions of doubt and unbelief. As we told others how bad things were, we were in reality cursing the people we loved. As we asked people to pray about this or that, we were gossiping. "I'm only telling you this so that you'll know how to pray," became a preamble to many conversations.

What we called prayer was a verbal listing of the evil we saw around us. Instead of praying, we spent hours in fervent worry!

PRAYER IS

There are many forms of prayer. Almost as many forms as there are Christians and situations. One form isn't "right" and another "wrong." One form isn't better than another. God's desire is that we operate in all of them at different times, as He leads us.

Many different words are used for prayer in the Bible.

Talking to God

Prayer is the simplest form of expression in the Christian life. It's talking to God. It can be a believer in child-like faith whispering the Father's name from their innermost being.

Galatians 4:6 And because you are sons, God has sent forth the Spirit of His Son into your hearts, crying out, "Abba, Father!"

Asking or Making a Request

Prayer is asking God for needed blessings, or expressing to Him our desires or longings.

1 Chronicles 4:10 And Jabez called on the God of Israel saying, "Oh, that You would bless me indeed, and enlarge my territory, that Your hand would be with me, and that You would keep me from evil, that I may not cause pain!" So God granted him what he requested.

Jesus said we were to ask.

Matthew 21:22 "And all things, whatever you ask in prayer, believing, you will receive."

John 16:23b,24 "Most assuredly, I say to you, whatever you ask the Father in My name He will give you. Until now you have asked nothing in My name. Ask, and you will receive, that your joy may be full."

Making Petition

The word "petition" means to cry out for help. When we petition God, we recognize that we are unable to meet our own needs and are depending on God's help.

1 Samuel 1:17 Then Eli answered and said, "Go in peace, and the God of Israel grant your petition which you have asked of Him."

Making Supplication

Prayer is supplication which means to ask for humbly, or earnestly.

1 Kings 8:33 When Your people Israel are defeated before an enemy because they have sinned against You, and when they turn back to You and confess Your name, and pray and make supplication to You in this temple ...

Entreating

Prayer can be in the form of entreaty and means to ask earnestly or to implore.

Exodus 8:8a Then Pharaoh called for Moses and Aaron, and said, "Entreat the LORD that He may take away the frogs from me and from my people ..."

Making Intercession

Prayer is intercession which is usually prayer on another's behalf.

Isaiah 53:12 Therefore I will divide Him a portion with the great, and He shall divide the spoil with the strong, because He poured out His soul unto death, and He was numbered with the transgressors, and He bore the sin of many, and made intercession for the transgressors.

An Act of Worship

In the book of Revelation, prayer is not only referred to as incense but is also offered with incense. The burning of incense is an act of worship representing the prayers of the saints.

Revelations 5:8 Now when He had taken the scroll, the four living creatures and the twenty-four elders fell down before the Lamb, each having a harp, and golden bowls full of incense, which are the prayers of the saints.

How awesome it is that the prayers of saints are stored in golden bowls in heaven! Which prayers are worthy of being preserved? Surely not a listing of errors, sins, complaints, worry, and selfishness. But rather, prayers like the prayer of Jesus as He hung on the cross.

Luke 23:34a Then Jesus said, "Father, forgive them, for they do not know what they do."

Certainly the prayer of Stephen as he was being martyred must be stored in heaven as an act of worship.

Acts 7:59,60 And they stoned Stephen as he was calling on God and saying, "Lord Jesus, receive my spirit." Then he knelt down and cried out with a loud voice, "Lord, do not charge them with this sin." And when he had said this, he fell asleep.

A Service

Anna – Seated at his feet Was a woman of Worship + prayer

There is a very real service to God in praying for His people.

Luke 2:37 And this woman was a widow of about eighty-four years, who did not depart from the temple, but served God with fastings and prayers night and day.

The apostle Paul wrote of Epaphras laboring in prayer.

Colossians 4:12 Epaphras, who is one of you, a servant of Christ, greets you, always laboring fervently for you in prayers, that you may stand perfect and complete in all the will of God.

Communion with God

God created Adam and Eve to have communion with Himself. He came down in the cool of the day and walked with them until sin entered the picture. From that day until now, there has been a desire deep within every human being to walk and talk with God.

Prayer is communion with God. Just as God speaks to man through His Word and by His Spirit, man speaks to God in prayer.

"Communion" means to share our deepest thoughts, longings, and feelings with one another. It means to have a two-way conversation.

Have you ever spent time with a person who talked non-stop about themselves – their job, family, house, car, problems – and never wanted to know one thing you were thinking or feeling? After a time, you began to wonder why you were there.

That's the way many of us behave toward God. We have our list to go over and spend our time in a one-way monologue. Then, just as God starts to answer, we realize we have run out of time and rush away. To have communion with God, we must talk to Him and let Him talk to us.

An Endless List

Our God is a God of endless variety – not even two snowflakes are the same. The ways we can pray are also endless.

Psalms is a marvelous book on prayer and speaks of prayer as crying to God, calling on God, waiting on God, and lifting up hands to God.

There are prayers of agreement, faith, deliverance, warfare, authority and more. All true prayers delight God.

Proverbs 15:8b ... but the prayer of the upright is His delight.

A Simple Definition

Let's consider a very simplified definition of prayer.

Prayer is taking a situation before the Lord, hearing His answer, and speaking God's will forth into the situation. Prayer is bringing heaven to earth.

THE TWO LANGUAGES OF PRAYER

The Spirit – The Understanding

The apostle Paul wrote about two languages of prayer – with the spirit and with the understanding.

1 Corinthians 14:14,15a For if I pray in a tongue, my spirit prays, but my understanding is unfruitful. What is the result then? I will pray with the spirit, and I will also pray with the understanding.

Paul prayed in the spirit and then he prayed with the understanding. Does this mean he prayed one way or another, or that he prayed first with the spirit and then with the understanding?

In Ephesians, he wrote about our armor, and we often stop with that in our understanding. However, the same passage has much to say about prayer.

Ephesians 6:17-20 And take the helmet of salvation, and the sword of the Spirit, which is the word of God; praying always with all prayer and supplication in the Spirit, being watchful to this end with all perseverance and supplication for all the saints – and for me, that utterance may be given to me, that I may open my mouth boldly to make known the mystery of the gospel, for which I am an ambassador in chains; that in it I may speak boldly, as I ought to speak.

The apostle Paul said we are to take the helmet of salvation and the Word of God with us and pray in the spirit. Why? He personalized it. "That utterance may be given to me ... that I may speak boldly as I ought to speak."

When we take the Word of God and pray in the spirit, our understanding becomes fruitful. Our minds receive revelation from God. Our minds become enlightened and then we can boldly and correctly pray with our understanding.

The Holy Spirit in Us

➤ *Grace and Supplication*

When Zechariah prophesied the coming of the Holy Spirit. He referred to Him as the Spirit of grace and supplication – unmerited favor and prayer.

➤ *That We May Know*

Zechariah 12:10a "And I will pour on the house of David and on the inhabitants of Jerusalem the Spirit of grace and supplication ..."

The apostle Paul wrote,
1 Corinthians 2:12,14 Now we have received, not the spirit of the world, but the Spirit who is from God, that we might know the things that have been freely given to us by God.

But the natural man does not receive the things of the Spirit of God, for they are foolishness to him; nor can he know them, because they are spiritually discerned.

The apostle John wrote,
John 16:13 "However, when He, the Spirit of truth, has come, He will guide you into all truth; for He will not speak on His own authority, but whatever He hears He will speak; and He will tell you things to come."

➤ *Pray in the Holy Spirit*

In the book of Jude we find,
Jude 1:20 But you, beloved, building yourselves up on your most holy faith, praying in the Holy Spirit ...

Paul wrote,
Ephesians 6:18 (NIV) And pray in the Spirit on all occasions with all kinds of prayers and requests. With this in mind, be alert and always keep on praying for all the saints.

The question comes up – can we pray in the spirit in our natural language? Yes, it's possible. We know we are doing this when we hear ourselves praying things we couldn't know.

The first time this happened to me, I was praying with a co-worker when I began to forcefully command the scars of the bankruptcy to be removed. I didn't know in the natural she had ever been involved in a bankruptcy. When I finished praying, we looked at each other. I was thinking, "What if there was no bankruptcy." Her first words were, "I didn't know you knew about the bankruptcy."

➤ *Prayer and Gifts of Holy Spirit*

7 Characters g the
Holy Spirit
1
2t. Wisdom
3 t. Knowledge/Understanding
4 t. Counsel
5 t. Might
6 t. Knowledge
7 t. reverence/fear of the Lord

It's so powerful when we pray and allow the gifts of the Holy Spirit to flow freely within us! Usually, we pray things we don't know naturally after we have spent time praying in the spirit – in tongues. This knowledge may come through the gift of tongues and interpretation, the word of knowledge, or the word of wisdom.

The gifts of the Holy Spirit are in operation when suddenly we know something we didn't know before. We know exactly how to pray, and because we have just heard from God so personally about the situation, our faith is supernaturally strong. When we operate in the gift of faith, miracles take place.

➤ *Groanings That Cannot Be Uttered*

The apostle Paul wrote,
Romans 8:26,27 Likewise the Spirit also helps in our weaknesses. For we do not know what we should pray for as we ought, but the Spirit Himself makes intercession for us with groanings which cannot be uttered. Now He who searches the hearts knows what the mind of the Spirit is, because He makes intercession for the saints according to the will of God.

Have you ever had something happen that hurt so terribly there was no way you could put it into words? Physically, you just dropped to your chair, to your knees, or even to the floor. Deep within there was a desire to pray, but you hurt too much to put it into words. After a time, you realized that beyond words, beyond your human understanding, there was a communication between you and God. This is the groaning that cannot be uttered. The Holy Spirit takes over for you, and then you begin to feel peace coming from your innermost being.

➤ *Springs and Rivers of Living Water*

This is the flow of the Holy Spirit through believers John was speaking about when he wrote,

John 7:38,39a (Amp) He who believes in Me – who cleaves to *and* trusts in *and* relies on Me – as the Scripture has said, Out from his innermost being springs *and* rivers of living water shall flow (continously). But He was speaking here of the Spirit ...

THE IMPORTANCE OF PRAYER

Greatest Privilege

Prayer is the greatest privilege of the Christian life, and privileges always bring responsibility. Blessings come in answer to prayer, and the promises of "whatsoever," "anything," and "all things," are for those who pray. God has given His people the wonderful opportunity of commanding His blessing on others and on themselves. What a responsibility we have, and what a loss to others and to ourselves when we don't pray.

Jesus Said to Pray

Jesus said we were to pray.
Matthew 6:6 "But you, when you pray, go into your room, and when you have shut your door, pray to your Father who is in the secret place; and your Father who sees in secret will reward you openly."

Jesus did not say, "if you pray." He said, "when you pray." He assumed the disciples, and we, would pray.

Great Men Prayed

Every verse or incident in the Bible is there for a reason and we have recorded prayers of Abraham, Moses, Elijah, Elisha, Hezekiah, Jeremiah, Daniel, Jonah, Manasseh, Nehemiah, Jabez, Epaphras, Paul, and the most important of all, Jesus.

The Early Church Prayed

In the early church, prayer had a very important place.

Acts 1:14 These all continued with one accord in prayer and supplication ...

Acts 2:42 And they continued steadfastly in the apostles' doctrine and fellowship, in the breaking of bread, and in prayers.

Acts 12:5,12 Peter was therefore kept in prison, but constant prayer was offered to God for him by the church.

So, when he had considered this, he came to the house of Mary ... where many were gathered together praying.

Acts 13:1,3 Now in the church that was at Antioch there were certain prophets and teachersl ... Then, having fasted and prayed, and laid hands on them, they sent them away.

✦ **Summary – What is Prayer?**

Prayer is not begging a reluctant God to act on our behalf. It's not a time of telling God all our problems. It's not convincing God of our worthiness or someone else's. It is not even a way to convince others of how spiritual we are.

Prayer is a time of communing with God – of talking to Him and listening to His reply just as we would with a very gracious, wonderful friend. Prayer is a time of coming to Him with our needs and the needs of others.

God has provided two ways for us to pray – with the spirit and with the understanding. He has given us the ability to pray with the spirit until our understanding is enlightened so that we can pray His will into our situations.

Prayer is both the privilege and responsibility of every believer.

QUESTIONS FOR REVIEW

1. Write your own definition of prayer using at least two scriptural references to support your position.

2. What are the two languages of prayer mentioned by the apostle Paul? Describe how they flow together.

3. Why is prayer important to you?

Lesson Two

Understanding the Basics

Before we can pray effectively, we must understand who can pray – what our position is in Christ – and what our authority is.

WHO CAN PRAY?

A prayer for salvation – of belief in Jesus, as the Son of God – is always heard. The thief dying on the cross prayed and was answered.

Luke 23:42,43 Then he said to Jesus, "Lord, remember me when You come into Your kingdom."

And Jesus said to him, "Assuredly, I say to you, today you will be with Me in Paradise."

The tax collector prayed and was heard.

Luke 18:13 And the tax collector, standing afar off, would not so much as raise his eyes to heaven, but beat his breast, saying, 'God be merciful to me a sinner!'

Prayer is the wondrous privilege of the children of God. We have the right to approach God in prayer. Let's look at some examples of who can pray from the Scriptures and then we will study our God-given position and authority.

Examples from Scripture

Race makes no difference. Financial success makes no difference. God hears people who call on His name, people who humble themselves, people who delight themselves in Him, people who commit their way to the Lord.

➢ *People of God*

2 Chronicles 7:14 "if My people who are called by My name will humble themselves, and pray and seek My face, and turn from their wicked ways, then I will hear from heaven, and will forgive their sin and heal their land. "

➢ *Those Who Delight in the Lord*

Psalms 37:4 Delight yourself also in the LORD, And He shall give you the desires of your heart.

➢ *Those Who Trust Him*

Psalms 37:5 Commit your way to the LORD, Trust also in Him, And He shall bring it to pass.

➢ *The Humble*

Psalms 10:17 LORD, You have heard the desire of the humble; You will prepare their heart; You will cause Your ear to hear.

➤ *The Poor and Destitute*

Psalms 69:33a For the LORD hears the poor ...

Psalms 102:17 He shall regard the prayer of the destitute, And shall not despise their prayer.

➤ *The Suffering*

James 5:13a Is anyone among you suffering? Let him pray.

➤ *The Oppressed*

Isaiah 19:20 And it will be for a sign and for a witness to the LORD of hosts in the land of Egypt; for they will cry to the LORD because of the oppressors, and He will send them a Savior and a Mighty One, and He will deliver them.

James 5:4 Indeed the wages of the laborers who mowed your fields, which you kept back by fraud, cry out; and the cries of the reapers have reached the ears of the Lord of Sabaoth.

➤ *Widows and Fatherless*

Exodus 22:22,23 You shall not afflict any widow or fatherless child. If you afflict them in any way, and they cry at all to Me, I will surely hear their cry.

➤ *Any Lacking Wisdom*

James 1:5 If any of you lacks wisdom, let him ask of God, who gives to all liberally and without reproach, and it will be given to him.

➤ *Seekers after Truth*

Acts 10:30,31 And Cornelius said, "Four days ago I was fasting until this hour; and at the ninth hour I prayed in my house, and behold, a man stood before me in bright clothing, and said, `Cornelius, your prayer has been heard, and your alms are remembered in the sight of God.'"

➤ *The Righteous*

Proverbs 15:29 The LORD is far from the wicked, but He hears the prayer of the righteous.

OUR POSITION IN CHRIST

To understand how we are to pray, we must first understand our position in Christ. For too many years, we have come to God as "poor lost sinners." We have come to Him with feelings of unworthiness and condemnation. We have seen ourselves as so destitute, that there was no way we could believe God would care about us, hear us, or work through us. That isn't how God sees us.

We were poor lost sinners, but through Christ we have been bought from the slave market of sin. We have been made a chosen generation, a royal priesthood. When we pray, we are to see ourselves from this position.

Sin Always a Barrier

➤ *Sacrifices Established*

When Adam and Eve sinned, they no longer had open communion with God. They were forced to leave the Garden of Eden where they had been able to walk and talk with God face to face. God made the first blood sacrifice to give them a covering.

Genesis 3:8-10,21 And they heard the sound of the LORD God walking in the garden in the cool of the day, and Adam and his wife hid themselves from the presence of the LORD God among the trees of the garden.

Then the LORD God called to Adam and said to him, "Where are you?"

So he said, "I heard Your voice in the garden, and I was afraid because I was naked; and I hid myself."

Also for Adam and his wife the LORD God made tunics of skin, and clothed them.

In Genesis four, we find the story of Cain and Abel making offerings – sacrifices – to the Lord. One was accepted, the other wasn't. Why? Cain had come into the presence of the Lord without the shedding of blood.

Genesis 4:2b-5a Now Abel was a keeper of sheep, but Cain was a tiller of the ground. And in the process of time it came to pass that Cain brought an offering of the fruit of the ground to the LORD. Abel also brought of the firstlings of his flock and of their fat. And the LORD respected Abel and his offering, but He did not respect Cain and his offering.

Through Moses, the law was given and God set up different sacrifices for different sins. But always, throughout Old Testament times, throughout the Old Covenant, God provided a way for men and women to approach Him through sacrifices – through shedding the blood of innocent animals.

All of the sacrifices pointed forward to the Perfect Sacrifice – the coming Lamb of God.

➤ *Priests Established*

God established the priests to be mediators between the people and God. They offered sacrifices for the people. God set in place the High Priest, the priest who once a year could come into the Holy of Holies and approach the mercy seat. He could, after making the proper sacrifices, come into the presence of God on behalf of the people.

Exodus 25:17,21,22a "You shall make a mercy seat of pure gold; two and a half cubits shall be its length and a cubit and a half its width.

"You shall put the mercy seat on top of the ark, and in the ark you shall put the Testimony that I will give you. And there I will meet with you, and I will speak with you ..."

The works of the priests pointed forward to Jesus Who became our High Priest.

Jesus Became

➤ *Our Sacrifice*

When Jesus died on the cross, He became the perfect, the complete Sacrifice for our sins. He removed the penalty of sin.

Hebrews 9:26b-28a ... but now, once at the end of the ages, He has appeared to put away sin by the sacrifice of Himself. And as it is appointed for men to die once, but after this the judgment, so Christ was offered once to bear the sins of many.

Hebrews 10:12-14 But this Man, after He had offered one sacrifice for sins forever, sat down at the right hand of God, from that time waiting till His enemies are made His footstool. For by one offering He has perfected forever those who are being sanctified.

➤ *Our High Priest*

The epistle to the Hebrews shows how Christ, by His own blood, became our High Priest, and opened the way for every believer to come into the presence of God.

Hebrews 2:17 Therefore, in all things He had to be made like His brethren, that He might be a merciful and faithful High Priest in things pertaining to God, to make propitiation for the sins of the people.

Hebrews 9:11,14 But Christ came as High Priest of the good things to come, with the greater and more perfect tabernacle not made with hands, that is, not of this creation.

How much more shall the blood of Christ, who through the eternal Spirit offered Himself without spot to God, purge your conscience from dead works to serve the living God?

➤ *Our Way*

John 14:6 Jesus said to him, "I am the way, the truth, and the life. No one comes to the Father except through Me."

There was a heavy veil in the temple which separated the Holy Place – where the priests could minister – from the Holy of Holies – the place where only the High Priest could minister. This veil symbolized the separation between the presence of God and mankind. The only way the High Priest could come into the presence of God was through this veil once a year.

At the moment Jesus died on the cross, this veil was supernaturally torn from top to bottom.

Matthew 27:50,51a Jesus, when He had cried out again with a loud voice, yielded up His spirit. And behold, the veil of the temple was torn in two from top to bottom ...

Today, the way we come into the presence of God is still through the veil – through Jesus, by the Spirit of God. We are no longer required to wait until the Day of Atonement. We are no longer required to bring a sacrifice for our sins to the priest and have him go in for us. We are required just as the priests of old, to come in faith with pure hearts.

Hebrews 10:18-22 Now where there is remission of these, there is no longer an offering for sin.

Therefore, brethren, having boldness to enter the Holiest by the blood of Jesus, by a new and living way which He consecrated for us, through the veil, that is, His flesh, and having a High Priest over the house of God, let us draw near with a true heart in full assurance of faith, having our hearts sprinkled from an evil conscience and our bodies washed with pure water.

Through the Sacrifice of Jesus

It will take the rest of our lives to understand all that Jesus did for us when He became our sacrifice. He took our shame. He took our curse. He paid the penalty for our sin. He made us new creations! Now, we can boldly enter into the presence of God as His sons and daughters.

➢ *We Are Bought*

We have been bought at a great price so that we can bring glory to God.

1 Corinthians 6:19,20 Or do you not know that your body is the temple of the Holy Spirit who is in you, whom you have from God, and you are not your own? For you were bought at a price; therefore glorify God in your body and in your spirit, which are God's.

➢ *Made A Chosen Generation*

We aren't to approach God as "poor lost sinners." That's what we were. Now, every believer is part of a chosen generation – a royal priesthood – a holy nation — a special people!

1 Peter 2:9 But you are a chosen generation, a royal priesthood, a holy nation, His own special people, that you may proclaim the praises of Him who called you out of darkness into His marvelous light.

➢ *Become Kings and Priests*

Peter referred to believers as a royal or kingly priesthood.

1 Peter 2:9 But you are a chosen generation, a royal priesthood ...

The apostle John wrote in Revelation that Jesus has made us kings and priests to His God and Father.

Revelation 1:5b,6 To Him who loved us and washed us from our sins in His own blood, and has made us kings and priests to His God and Father, to Him be glory and dominion forever and ever. Amen.

It is important that we are called priests and kings.

➥ **A priest makes intercession and a king rules.**

➥ **A priest asks for, intercedes, and stands between an unholy people and a righteous God.**

➥ **A king prays authoritative, ruling prayers.**

When Jesus cried out over the sins of Jerusalem, He was operating as the Priest and is our example of being priests.

Matthew 23:37 "O Jerusalem, Jerusalem, the one who kills the prophets and stones those who are sent to her! How often I wanted to gather your children together, as a hen gathers her chicks under her wings, but you were not willing!"

When He stood in the midst of the storm and said, "Peace be still." He was operating as the King and is our example of operating as kings over this earth.

Mark 4:39 Then He arose and rebuked the wind, and said to the sea, "Peace, be still!" And the wind ceased and there was a great calm.

➤ *Can Boldly Enter In*

The writer of the book of Hebrews tells us we are to be bold in entering into the Holy of Holies through the blood of Jesus.

Hebrews 10:19 Therefore, brethren, having boldness to enter the Holiest by the blood of Jesus ...

What Is Our Position?

Every believer walking in faith and obedience, has the right to enter into God's presence on the grounds of redemption by the blood of Jesus and through Jesus our High Priest. It's because of this we are told to come with boldness and with full assurance of faith.

Hebrews 10:22 Let us draw near with a true heart in full assurance of faith, having our hearts sprinkled from an evil conscience and our bodies washed with pure water.

Hebrews 4:16 Let us therefore come boldly to the throne of grace, that we may obtain mercy and find grace to help in time of need.

It's those who give the right place and value to the blood of Christ who can approach God boldly and confidently in prayer.

OUR AUTHORITY IN CHRIST

Many ask, "If God is sovereign and can do anything in the world He wants to do, why should we pray?

"Why doesn't God just drive evil out of earth as He did in heaven?

"Perhaps, if we pray long enough, or hard enough, or sincerely enough, or if we cry enough, we can convince God to act on our behalf.

"For some reason, God seems reluctant to act on earth, but maybe our prayers can convince Him to do so. Why doesn't God act sovereignly in our situation?

"Maybe He doesn't understand it, and we should tell Him about it over and over – remind Him until He does what we desire."

Who Is God?

Shirley Guthrie wrote, "God is not a Great Heavenly Granddaddy who does everything for us and makes our lives smooth and painless and easy. Nor is He a Great Heavenly Tyrant who terrorizes us by His arbitrary, unpredictable, power and glory.

"The Bible does tell us two things about the living and Sovereign God. On the one hand, He is in fact infinite, almighty, sovereign, sufficient in Himself, able to do whatever He pleases. And on the other hand, He is in fact a God who draws near to men and makes Himself known in an intimate way as the God who will help and be their companion.

"He is neither a Tyrant, nor a Granddaddy, nor a combination of both. But He is in fact a God who is both free from mankind and yet bound to them; far above, yet with them; distant, yet near; powerful and yet loving, loving and yet powerful at the same time."

*Note: The above quotes are taken from **Christian Doctrine** Published by CLC Press, Richmond, Virginia.*

When we try to understand God, we find our human minds are far too small to ever do so. We tend to focus on just a few aspects. God is so much more than we will ever understand!

➢ *God's Sovereignty*

God is sovereign. This is a term which expresses the supreme rulership of God. God is absolute. He is under no external restraint whatsoever. All forms of existence are within the scope of His dominion.

God has only the restraints He places on Himself and the restraints His character places on Himself. For example, God is perfect Love and so He will not do anything that will violate that perfect Love.

Who Is Man?

David does a wonderful job of explaining to us about God and mankind.

Psalms 8:4-9 What is man that You are mindful of him, And the son of man that You visit him?

For You have made him a little lower than the angels, And You have crowned him with glory and honor.

You have made him to have dominion over the works of Your hands; You have put all things under his feet,

All sheep and oxen – Even the beasts of the field,

The birds of the air, And the fish of the sea That pass through the paths of the seas.

O LORD, our Lord, How excellent is Your name in all the earth!

Delegated Authority

When God created Adam and Eve in His image, He created them on the same planet where Satan and all of his demons were cast when they were thrown out of heaven. The first thing He said about Adam and Eve, after He created them was, "Let them have dominion."

Genesis 1:26,27 Then God said, "Let Us make man in Our image, according to Our likeness; let them have dominion over the fish of the sea, over the birds of the air, and over the cattle, over all the earth and over every creeping thing that creeps on the earth."

So God created man in His own image; in the image of God He created him; male and female He created them.

On earth, this all powerful, Almighty One delegated His dominion to mankind. He placed His dominion over this earth in their hands!

Dominion means to subjugate, to bring under control, to conquer, to enslave.

What on earth, a perfect earth recreated by God, needed to be controlled, conquered, and enslaved? Satan and his demons.

Even when Adam and Eve sinned, God didn't take back the authority He had given them. Mankind surrendered it to Satan and Satan became the god of this world. For two thousand years, Satan held this authority and no matter how terrible things became God didn't take it back.

Why? Because He had delegated it to mankind.

The Last Adam

When we begin to understand who the first Adam was – who he was created to be – we can begin to understand why it's important to us that Jesus came as the Last Adam.

The first Adam was created to walk in authority on this earth. He was created to take dominion over Satan and his demons. He was created to have fellowship with God.

Jesus came as the Last Adam – the prefect Human Being. Jesus came to walk in authority over this earth, to resist Satan, to live a perfect life, and to die as our substitute – the perfect Sacrifice.

1 Corinthians 15:45 And so it is written, "The first man Adam became a living being." The last Adam became a life-giving spirit.

We must realize that Jesus didn't operate on earth, in His power as the Son of God. He laid aside those rights and operated on earth as a Man – a perfect Man – the Man God had created Adam to be.

Philippians 2:6-8 ... who, being in the form of God, did not consider it robbery to be equal with God, but made Himself of no reputation, taking the form of a servant, and coming in the likeness of men. And being found in appearance as a man, He humbled Himself and became obedient to the point of death, even the death of the cross.

When Jesus stood in the boat and said to the elements, "Peace, be still!" there was a great calm. That was dominion!

In death, Jesus defeated Satan, took back the keys, and gave them to believers, to His body, to His church.

Matthew 16:19 "And I will give you the keys of the kingdom of heaven, and whatever you bind on earth will be bound in heaven, and whatever you loose on earth will be loosed in heaven."

Jesus said He was going to build a church and that the gates of Hades wouldn't prevail against it. Jesus said whatever we would bind on earth, would be bound in heaven and whatever we loosed on earth would be loosed in heaven.

Jesus described this delegated authority in Mark.

Mark 13:34 It is like a man going to a far country, who left his house and gave authority to his servants, and to each his work, and commanded the doorkeeper to watch.

When we pray, we release the power and the authority of God to work on earth. In heaven, God has all authority, but on earth, He's given His authority to the church – to you and me.

The authority that is to be exercised on this planet must come from those who are in Christ!

Free Volition

Just as God gave mankind dominion and authority on this earth, He gave them free volition. And just as God will not violate the realms of authority He has given to humanity, He will not violate our free volition.

Volition is simply the right to choose. Adam and Eve were given the right to choose between obeying God or disobeying.

God has never taken away this right which He gave to all humanity through Adam and Eve. We have the right to choose. We can believe in God or not believe in Him. We can love Him, or not love Him. We can serve Him, or not serve Him. The choices concerning what we do every minute of every day is ours. The responsibility for what happens because of these choices is also ours.

How often do we hear believers question, "How could God let such an awful thing happen?"

God didn't allow it to happen. We did.

This truth isn't to bring condemnation. It's to bring liberty. Iniquity has piled up one generation on another. Evil has multiplied to the point that the truth seems almost to be buried. But God's Word is still true. The authority on this earth belongs to us. Jesus took it back for us. He gave us the keys of authority. The only thing Satan or his demons can do on this earth is what humanity has been letting them do. It's time we become bold in Jesus Christ. We must learn to pray and take dominion with our restored authority.

In His Name

Our position and our authority are completely in Jesus. Therefore we must always pray to the Father in Jesus' name. We are accepted in Jesus; we are beloved in Him; we are joint heirs with Him. Everything we have is in Jesus.

John 14:6,13 Jesus said to him, "I am the way, the truth, and the life. No one comes to the Father except through Me.

And whatever you ask in My name, that I will do, that the Father may be glorified in the Son."

◆ Summary – Understanding the Basics

God created Adam and Eve to have fellowship with Him. He came during the cool of the day just to talk with them, but that superb relationship was lost when Adam and Eve sinned. The authority He had delegated to them was surrendered to Satan who became the ruler of this world. God could have turned His back and left this planet and everything on it in the control of Satan – but He didn't.

The Son of God, Jesus, came to take back from Satan all that humanity had lost. Jesus laid aside His rights as God and came to earth as the Last Adam. He walked on this earth in authority as men and women were created to walk. He died on the cross to pay the penalty for sin. Through His sacrifice we became part of the chosen generation – chosen in Him. In Him, we became kings and priests. He gave us His name and He gave us His authority.

QUESTIONS FOR REVIEW

1. In your own words, explain authority, delegated authority, and free volition.

2. On what grounds does every believer have a right to enter God's presence and make requests?

3. Why doesn't God just see a person's needs and send the right blessing at the right time without them having to ask?

Jesus Prayed

Jesus is our example in every area of our Christian walk. To know what we are to do, we should study what He did. During the earthly ministry of Jesus, the people came to Him. They asked of Him and He met their needs. He set them free from demon bondage. He healed their bodies.

Jesus was a man of prayer. He prayed and He taught His disciples to pray.

JESUS ANSWERED PRAYERS OF NEEDY PEOPLE

Jesus answered the requests of the people wherever He went during His time of ministry on this earth. There is great encouragement for us in these answers. We will look at only a few of these prayers and the answers.

I'm Willing

A leper came to Jesus and said, "If You are willing, You can make me clean."

How exciting Jesus' answer is, "I'm willing!" He expressed the heart of the Father when He said, "I'm willing!"

Mark 1:40-42 Then a leper came to Him, imploring Him, kneeling down to Him and saying to Him, "If You are willing, You can make me clean."

And Jesus, moved with compassion, put out His hand and touched him, and said to him, "I am willing; be cleansed."

As soon as He had spoken, immediately the leprosy left him, and he was cleansed.

If our prayer is for healing, God is still willing.

Only Believe

We have another example of an answer to prayer for healing when a ruler of the synagogue fell at Jesus' feet and begged Him earnestly for his daughter's life. Even as he asked, the worst news possible came. "It's too late. Your daughter is dead."

But Jesus spoke, "Don't be afraid, only believe." What a challenge to us. When we have prayed and all hope is gone, we are still to believe.

Mark 5:22,23,35-42 And behold, one of the rulers of the synagogue came, Jairus by name. And when he saw Him, he fell at His feet and begged Him earnestly, saying, "My little daughter lies at the point of death. Come and lay Your hands on her, that she may be healed, and she will live."

While He (Jesus) was still speaking, some came from the ruler of the synagogue's house who said, "Your daughter is dead. Why trouble the Teacher any further?"

As soon as Jesus heard the word that was spoken, He said to the ruler of the synagogue, "Do not be afraid; only believe."

And He permitted no one to follow Him except Peter, James, and John the brother of James. Then He came to the house of the ruler of the synagogue, and saw a tumult and those who wept and wailed loudly. When He came in, He said to them, "Why make this commotion and weep? The child is not dead, but sleeping." And they laughed Him to scorn.

But when He had put them all out, He took the father and the mother of the child, and those who were with Him, and entered where the child was lying. Then He took the child by the hand, and said to her, "Talitha, cumi," which is translated, "Little girl, I say to you, arise."

Immediately the girl arose and walked, for she was twelve years of age. And they were overcome with great amazement.

According to Your Faith

Two blind men knew to cry out to Jesus.

Matthew 9:27-30a When Jesus departed from there, two blind men followed Him, crying out and saying, "Son of David, have mercy on us!"

And when He had come into the house, the blind men came to Him. And Jesus said to them, "Do you believe that I am able to do this?" They said to Him, "Yes, Lord."

Then He touched their eyes, saying, "According to your faith let it be to you." And their eyes were opened.

Be Specific

Two blind men sat by the roadside begging. When Jesus came by, they called out, "O Lord, have mercy on us!"

Jesus answered, "What do you want Me to do?" Were they asking for money or were they asking for healing?

Matthew 20:29-34 Now as they departed from Jericho, a great multitude followed Him. And behold, two blind men sitting by the road, when they heard that Jesus was passing by, cried out, saying, "Have mercy on us, O Lord, Son of David!"

Then the multitude warned them that they should be quiet; but they cried out all the more, saying, "Have mercy on us, O Lord, Son of David!"

So Jesus stood still and called them, and said, "What do you want Me to do for you?"

They said to Him, "Lord, that our eyes may be opened."

So Jesus had compassion and touched their eyes. And immediately their eyes received sight, and they followed Him.

Notice that when those around them said, "Be quiet! Leave Him alone," they continued in their requests. However, they still weren't specific enough. In this example, there are two truths for us. We need to continue to cry out to God for our needs even when others say to stop, and we need to be specific.

Rebuked the Demon

Matthew 17:14-21 And when they had come to the multitude, a man came to Him, kneeling down to Him and saying, "Lord, have mercy on my son, for he is an epileptic and suffers severely; for he often falls into the fire and often into the water. So I brought him to Your disciples, but they could not cure him."

Then Jesus answered and said, "O faithless and perverse generation, how long shall I be with you? How long shall I bear with you? Bring him here to Me." And Jesus rebuked the demon, and he came out of him; and the child was cured from that very hour.

Then the disciples came to Jesus privately and said, "Why could we not cast him out?"

So Jesus said to them, "Because of your unbelief; for assuredly, I say to you, if you have faith as a mustard seed, you will say to this mountain, 'Move from here to there,' and it will move; and nothing will be impossible for you. However, this kind does not go out except by prayer and fasting."

The disciples questioned Jesus about their lack of power in this situation and Jesus gave them the cause – their unbelief – and the solution – prayer and fasting.

THE PRAYER LIFE OF JESUS

Everything we have, everything we are, everything we are to do is through Jesus. If Jesus, the only Son of God, the Last Adam, the Perfect Man needed to spend time alone with God, how much more we need to do so.

What could be more important in a study on prayer than the prayers of Jesus. We find more of the prayer life of Jesus recorded in Luke than in the other Gospels.

Prayed at His Baptism

Jesus prayed at His baptism. We aren't told what He prayed only that He did pray and God responded.

Luke 3:21,22 Now when all the people were baptized, it came to pass that Jesus also was baptized; and while He prayed, the heaven was opened. And the Holy Spirit descended in bodily form like a dove upon Him, and a voice came from heaven which said, "You are My beloved Son; in You I am well pleased."

Prayed Alone in the Morning

Jesus prayed in the early morning in a solitary place.

Mark 1:35 Now in the morning, having risen a long while before daylight, He went out and departed to a solitary place; and there He prayed.

Prayed Before Making Decisions

Jesus prayed before He made major decisions.

Luke 6:12,13 Now it came to pass in those days that He went out to the mountain to pray, and continued all night in prayer to God. And when it was day, He called His disciples to Him; and from them He chose twelve whom He also named apostles.

Withdrew and Prayed

When the multitudes were all around Him, and many desired healing, Jesus often withdrew and prayed. The needs of the people, didn't keep Him from spending time in prayer.

Luke 5:15,16 Then the report went around concerning Him all the more; and great multitudes came together to hear, and to be healed by Him of their infirmities. So He Himself often withdrew into the wilderness and prayed.

Mark 6:46 And when He had sent them away, He departed to the mountain to pray.

Prayed Before Miracle

Jesus asked the Lord's blessing to be on the food and then He distributed it to the disciples and they to the multitude. Prayer was the first step in the miracle of feeding the 5,000.

Luke 9:16,17 Then He took the five loaves and the two fish, and looking up to heaven, He blessed and broke them, and gave them to the disciples to set before the multitude. So they all ate and were filled, and twelve baskets of the leftover fragments were taken up by them.

Prayed with Disciples

He prayed by Himself, and He prayed with others.

Luke 9:18a And it happened, as He was alone praying, that His disciples joined Him ...

Prayed for Little Children

He laid His hands on the little children and prayed for them.

Matthew 19:13a Then little children were brought to Him that He might put His hands on them and pray ...

Prayed for Simon by Name

He prayed for one of the disciples by name.

Luke 22:31,32 And the Lord said, "Simon, Simon! Indeed, Satan has asked for you, that he may sift you as wheat. But I have prayed for you, that your faith should not fail; and when you have returned to Me, strengthen your brethren."

His Face Was Transformed

One time when Jesus prayed, His face and His clothing were transformed.

Luke 9:28,29 And it came to pass, about eight days after these sayings, that He took Peter, John, and James and went up on the mountain to pray. And as He prayed, the appearance of His face was altered, and His robe became white and glistening.

Prayer of Rejoicing

In Luke we aren't only told that Jesus prayed, we are also told what He prayed.

Luke 10:21 In that hour Jesus rejoiced in the Spirit and said, "I praise You, Father, Lord of heaven and earth, that You have hidden these things from the wise and prudent and revealed them to babes. Even so, Father, for so it seemed good in Your sight."

JESUS PRAYED FOR US!

The whole chapter of John 17, gives us a marvelous prayer of Jesus. As His time on earth was drawing to an end, He prayed for the disciples, the believers of that time, and for those who would follow.

Glorify Me So I Can Glorify You

John 17:1-19 Jesus spoke these words, lifted up His eyes to heaven, and said: "Father, the hour has come. Glorify Your Son, that Your Son also may glorify You, as You have given Him authority over all flesh, that He should give eternal life to as many as You have given Him. And this is eternal life, that they may know You, the only true God, and Jesus Christ whom You have sent.

I Have Finished My Work

"I have glorified You on the earth. I have finished the work which You have given Me to do. And now, O Father, glorify Me together with Yourself, with the glory which I had with You before the world was.

I Have Manifested Your Name

"I have manifested Your name to the men whom You have given Me out of the world. They were Yours, You gave them to Me, and they have kept Your word. Now they have known that all things which You have given Me are from You.

I Have Given Them Your Word

"For I have given to them the words which You have given Me; and they have received them, and have known surely that I came forth from You; and they have believed that You sent Me.

I Pray for Them

"I pray for them. I do not pray for the world but for those whom You have given Me, for they are Yours. And all Mine are Yours, and Yours are Mine, and I am glorified in them.

➤ *Keep Them Through Your Name*

"Now I am no longer in the world, but these are in the world, and I come to You. Holy Father, keep through Your name those whom You have given Me, that they may be one as We are. While I was with them in the world, I kept them in Your name. Those whom You gave Me I have kept; and none of them is lost except the son of perdition, that the Scripture might be fulfilled.

➤ *That They May Have Joy*

"But now I come to You, and these things I speak in the world, that they may have My joy fulfilled in themselves. I have given them Your word; and the world has hated them because they are not of the world, just as I am not of the world.

➤ *Keep Them from the Evil One*

"I do not pray that You should take them out of the world, but that You should keep them from the evil one. They are not of the world, just as I am not of the world.

➤ *Sanctify Them*

"Sanctify them by Your truth. Your word is truth. As You sent Me into the world, I also have sent them into the world. And for their sakes I sanctify Myself, that they also may be sanctified by the truth."

He Prayed for Us!

Jesus' prayer continued for the disciples and believers of that time, and then He prayed for those who would follow. That includes us! Jesus, while He was on this earth, prayed for us.

➤ *Those Who Would Believe*

John 17:20-26 "I do not pray for these alone, but also for those who will believe in Me through their word.

➤ *For Unity of Believers*

"that they all may be one, as You, Father, are in Me, and I in You; that they also may be one in Us, that the world may believe that You sent Me.

➤ *To Have Glory*

"And the glory which You gave Me I have given them, that they may be one just as We are one:

➤ *To Be Made Perfect*

"I in them, and You in Me; that they may be made perfect in one, and that the world may know that You have sent Me, and have loved them as You have loved Me.

➤ *To One Day Be with Him*

"Father, I desire that they also whom You gave Me may be with Me where I am, that they may behold My glory which You have given Me; for You loved Me before the foundation of the world. O righteous Father! The world has not known You, but I have known You; and these have known that You sent Me.

➤ *To Be Filled with His Love*

"And I have declared to them Your name, and will declare it, that the love with which You loved Me may be in them, and I in them."

From this time of praying, Jesus and the disciples went immediately to the Garden of Gethsemane.

John 18:1 When Jesus had spoken these words, He went out with His disciples over the Brook Kidron, where there was a garden, which He and His disciples entered.

HIS PRAYERS CONTINUE

At Gethsemane

Jesus was facing death. He was in sorrow and deeply distressed and knew He must pray. It was His desire that the disciples pray with Him, but they failed. Most of us know what happened.

➢ *John's Account*

Jesus prayed in anguish.
John 12:27,28 "Now My soul is troubled, and what shall I say? 'Father, save Me from this hour'? But for this purpose I came to this hour. Father, glorify Your name." Then a voice came from heaven, saying, "I have both glorified it and will glorify it again."

➢ *Matthew's Account*

Mathew's account of this time shows us the humanity of Jesus. He desired the close bond of others lifting Him up in prayer. In His humanity, He was setting His will to do God's will even to death on the cross.

Matthew 26:36-46 Then Jesus came with them to a place called Gethsemane, and said to the disciples, "Sit here while I go and pray over there."

And He took with Him Peter and the two sons of Zebedee, and He began to be sorrowful and deeply distressed. Then He said to them, "My soul is exceedingly sorrowful, even to death. Stay here and watch with Me."

⇨ First Prayer

He went a little farther and fell on His face, and prayed, saying, "O My Father, if it is possible, let this cup pass from Me; nevertheless, not as I will, but as You will."

Jesus prayed, "Not as I will, but as You will."

Then He came to the disciples and found them asleep, and said to Peter, "What, could you not watch with Me one hour? Watch and pray, lest you enter into temptation. The spirit indeed is willing, but the flesh is weak."

When Jesus found them asleep, He asked, "Could you not watch with Me one hour? And then He told them why they were to pray – lest you enter into temptation – they would follow their own will.

⇨ Second Prayer

He went away again a second time and prayed, saying, "O My Father, if this cup cannot pass away from Me unless I drink it, Your will be done."

⇨ Third Prayer

Notice, the second time Jesus came and found them asleep – He let them sleep. He didn't warn them the second time.

And He came and found them asleep again, for their eyes were heavy. So He left them, went away again, and prayed the third time, saying the same words.

Jesus prayed the third time, "Your will be done."

Then He came to His disciples and said to them, "Are you still sleeping and resting? Behold, the hour is at hand, and the Son of Man is being betrayed into the hands of sinners. Rise, let us be going. See, he who betrays Me is at hand."

➤ *Luke's Account*

Luke, the doctor gives us a vivid picture of this time of prayer.

Luke 22:43,44 Then an angel appeared to Him from heaven, strengthening Him. And being in agony, He prayed more earnestly. And His sweat became like great drops of blood falling down to the ground.

On the Cross

➤ *Father Forgive Them*

Jesus' prayer as He hung on the cross has to be the most awesome in all Scripture. He was betrayed by His own creation. He was reviled, hated, and crucified by the very beings He had created. He was murdered by the ones to whom He had come to bring salvation. If any person on the face of the earth has ever had cause to not forgive, it was Jesus. And yet even as He hung in excruciating pain, dying, He prayed, "Father forgive them ..."

Luke 23:34a Then Jesus said, "Father, forgive them, for they do not know what they do."

➤ *His Last Cry*

Luke 23:46 And when Jesus had cried out with a loud voice, He said, "Father, 'into Your hands I commend My spirit.' " And having said this, He breathed His last.

Ever Lives to Make Intercession

Jesus was a man of prayer. An example to us of praying continuously. Today, He is still praying – He is making intercession for us in heaven.

Hebrews 7:25 Therefore He is also able to save to the uttermost those who come to God through Him, since He ever lives to make intercession for them.

✦ Summary – Jesus Our Great Example

Jesus as our Supreme Commander in Chief is also our example of how to live a victorious life of prayer and obedience. The Gospels are full of references to His life of prayer and give us insight into our relationship with our heavenly Father. That Jesus, the Son of God, prayed in every circumstance and situation is a challenge for us. Are we living our lives as we think they should be, or are we going continuously to our Father for direction?

Jesus prayed for us – for those who would believe – that we would walk in love and unity, be made perfect, that His glory would be seen in us, and that one day we would be with Him.

QUESTIONS FOR REVIEW

1. In response to the blind men asking for mercy in Matthew 20:27, why did Jesus ask them what they wanted Him to do for them? What did you learn about prayer from this scripture?

2. In Matthew 17:14, when the man with an epileptic son came to Jesus and said that His disciples couldn't cure him, what were the reasons Jesus gave the disciples privately as to why they couldn't do this? What did you learn about prayer from this scripture?

3. Give three other examples of Jesus' prayers and describe what you learned from these examples. Describe the changes you will make in your prayer life from truths learned from this lesson.

Lesson Four

"Lord, Teach Us to Pray"

The disciples saw that Jesus' life was one of prayer, and one day they said, "Lord, teach us to pray." There was something different in Jesus' life – there was something they needed.

Luke 11:1 And it came to pass, as He was praying in a certain place, when He ceased, that one of His disciples said to Him, "Lord, teach us to pray, as John also taught his disciples."

This should continuously be the prayer of our hearts,

"Lord, teach us to pray!"

THE LORD'S PRAYER

The Lord's Prayer was to be a model that the disciples were to use in formatting their own prayers. It wasn't to be repeated, as it has been for centuries, by rote in religious ceremonies.

Notice how short the prayer Jesus used as His example actually is – just three verses in Luke – or five verses in Matthew (6:9-13).

So He said to them, "When you pray, say:
Our Father in heaven, hallowed be Your name.
Your kingdom come.
Your will be done on earth as it is in heaven.

Give us day by day our daily bread.
and forgive us our sins,
for we also forgive everyone who is indebted to us.

And do not lead us into temptation,
but deliver us from the evil one."
Luke 11:2-4

Many splendid books have been written on these few verses, but we will focus only on the first verse.

"When You Pray – Say!"

In this prayer, Jesus didn't say when you pray, cry as you plead with a reluctant God to hear you, or to beg and agonize. He said when you pray – say.

Jesus used the same word, say, in another place.

Mark 11:23 "For assuredly, I say to you, whoever says to this mountain, 'Be removed and be cast into the sea,' and does not doubt in his heart, but believes that those things he says will come to pass, he will have whatever he says."

When we pray, we are to say. We are to say to the mountain – "Be thou removed and be cast into the sea." And Jesus said if we don't doubt, but believe we will have whatever we say, it will be done.

Remember our simplified definition of prayer is:

Prayer is taking a situation before the Lord, hearing His answer, and speaking forth God's will into the situation. Prayer is bringing heaven to earth.

"Our Father in Heaven"

➤ *Our Position*

Jesus reminded the disciples of their position. When we come to God in prayer, we are to come as children of the most high God. It's our covenant right to come to Him just as natural children run to their earthly parents.

Romans 8:15,16 For you did not receive the spirit of bondage again to fear, but you received the Spirit of adoption by whom we cry out, "Abba, Father."

We are to pray to our heavenly Father, realizing that He is totally different than our earthly father. We are to pray to our Father in heaven – not to the God within ourselves as some teach.

"Hallowed Be Your Name"

➤ *Our Attitude*

Then Jesus instructed the disciples about their attitude in prayer.

Even though we are God's beloved children, we don't rush into His presence with disrespect. We give Him honor. "Hallowed" means to make holy, to purify, to consecrate, to regard with respect or reverence, to appreciate, to hold dear, to cherish. We take time to hallow His name by saying things from our heart that reverence Him.

"Your Kingdom Come"

When we pray, we are to say "Your kingdom come" – not our kingdom. Many without realizing it, have been praying to build their own kingdoms – a nicer house, a bigger car, a better job, even a larger ministry. Jesus said we are to say – "God's kingdom come."

We are to put ourselves in agreement with God, and then command His will be done on earth in our situation. This is a kingly prayer, one of rulership.

➤ *Come – Ercomehe*

The Greek word, *ercomehe,* means, "to come from over there to over here."

It doesn't mean, "God's in charge and whatever will be, will be"

It doesn't mean, "It would be nice if ..., but whatever Your will is God."

When Jesus said "come" in the Greek language, it meant, "call those things that be not as though they were."

It meant, "You, come from over there to over here."

➤ *Walking on the Water*

Peter walked on the water in response to Jesus saying, *Ercomehe* – Come.

Matthew 14:28,29 And Peter answered Him and said, "Lord, if it is You, command me to come to You on the water."

So He said, "Come." And when Peter had come down out of the boat, he walked on the water to go to Jesus.

Peter was a fisherman. He knew humans don't walk on water. However, in response to his desire – "Lord command me to come to You on the water" – Jesus responded, "Come." Peter moved from the natural to the supernatural realm. Peter walked on the water.

After Peter was walking on the water, he began to move back into the natural realm, to be afraid, and then he started to sink.

Matthew 14:30,31 But when he saw that the wind was boisterous, he was afraid; and beginning to sink he cried out, saying, "Lord, save me!"

And immediately Jesus stretched out His hand and caught him, and said to him, "O you of little faith, why did you doubt?"

Often, it's the same today, as we move into the supernatural realm in prayer. We start out boldly, but then we begin to look at the circumstances. We let doubt come in. We become afraid and start to fail. At that moment our prayer should be the same as Peter's, "Lord save me – help me believe."

➤ *The Centurion*

The centurion came to Jesus pleading with Him to heal his servant, and Jesus said, "I will come and heal him." But the centurion knew it wasn't necessary for Jesus to come – that Jesus could just speak and the servant would be healed.

Matthew 8:5-10 Now when Jesus had entered Capernaum, a centurion came to Him, pleading with Him, saying, "Lord, my servant is lying at home paralyzed, dreadfully tormented."

And Jesus said to him, "I will come and heal him."

The centurion answered and said, "Lord, I am not worthy that You should come under my roof. But only speak a word and my servant will be healed."

The centurion went on to explain that since he was under authority, and had soldiers under his authority, he understood authority. He used the word, *ercomehe*.

"For I also am a man under authority, having soldiers under me. And I say to this one, 'Go,' and he goes; and to another, 'Come,' and he comes; and to my servant, 'Do this,' and he does it."

When Jesus heard it He marveled and said to those who followed, "Assuredly I say to you I have not found such great faith not even in Israel!"

We will never be able to understand speaking with authority, commanding, until we are under authority – until we are in true submission to the authority of God.

> *Come – A Command*

Ercomehe isn't a suggestion, it's a command. It's a calling forth with authority. "Your kingdom come!" The kingdom of God will not come until it's commanded to come. On earth, God has given that kind of authority to us.

This sample prayer that Jesus gave the disciples is built on an understanding of the authority that God gave to Adam and Eve. He didn't give some authority to them and hold back some for Himself, and Jesus didn't win back just some of our authority. He did a complete work.

"Your Will Be Done on Earth As It Is in Heaven"

This is an awesome part of the sample prayer Jesus gave us. "Your will be done on earth just as it's done in heaven."

What is God's will in heaven? What is His will on earth?

> *In Heaven*

In heaven, there is only one will and that is God's. There are no discussions about it. There are no choices to be made. God's will is done joyfully and automatically. In heaven, there is no dissension, just yes and amen to the will of God.

> *On Earth*

Jesus said we are to command God's will to be done on earth just as it is in heaven.

When Adam and Eve sinned, they exercised their wills contrary to God's and all humanity has done the same ever since that day.

For years, we prayed our will be done. "Lord, we need a new car, a new house, a job." We were seeking things – important things we needed – and praying for our will to be done.

Now we see Jesus not only as our Savior and Provider, but also as our Lord and King. We are submitting our will to Him so that we will no longer be saying, "Lord, I want ..."

God's will cannot be done in our corner of the earth until we, the body of Christ, say, "Lord, Your will be done on earth as it is in heaven." What an awesome prayer! We have the responsibility of being a covering over our families, our neighborhoods, our cities, and the countries where we live.

The devil came to kill, steal, and destroy. The reason he can do it in our realms of authority is because we haven't learned how to pray – what to say. We haven't learned how to release the power of God into our situations.

The more we understand how to release the will of God to be done in our realms of authority, the more exciting prayer becomes! The more we study God's Word and pray in the spirit, the more we will know how to speak forth God's will in our territories.

WHAT IS THE KINGDOM OF GOD?

Prophesied by Daniel

We are to speak God's kingdom into our situations. We are to say, "Your kingdom come." To do this more effectively, we must understand what the kingdom of God is.

Daniel 7:13,14,18,27 "I was watching in the night visions, and behold, One like the Son of Man, coming with the clouds of heaven! He came to the Ancient of Days, and they brought Him near before Him. Then to Him was given dominion and glory and a kingdom, that all peoples, nations, and languages should serve Him. His dominion is an everlasting dominion, which shall not pass away, and His kingdom the one which shall not be destroyed.

'But the saints of the Most High shall receive the kingdom, and possess the kingdom forever, even forever and ever.'

Then the kingdom and dominion, and the greatness of the kingdoms under the whole heaven, shall be given to the people, the saints of the Most High. His kingdom is an everlasting kingdom, and all dominions shall serve and obey Him."

☞ **From Daniel we learn that the kingdom is everlasting and it is the saints who receive it.**

Prophesied by John the Baptist

John knew the kingdom of God was at hand.

Matthew 3:2 and saying, "Repent, for the kingdom of heaven is at hand!"

☞ **The kingdom of God came to earth with the ministry of Jesus.**

Later in prison when John asked if Jesus was the One he had been prophesying about, Jesus sent back the answer.

Matthew 11:4,5 Jesus answered and said to them, "Go and tell John the things which you hear and see: The blind receive their sight and the lame walk; the lepers are cleansed and the deaf hear; the dead are raised up and the poor have the gospel preached to them."

Jesus sent John testimonies of the blind receiving their sight, the lame walking, the lepers being cleansed, the deaf hearing, the dead being raised up and the gospel being preached as proof that the kingdom of God had come.

Jesus Said and Did

Jesus mentioned the kingdom of God many times in addition to this reference in the Lord's Prayer. We can learn what the kingdom of God actually is through these scriptures.

➢ *Jesus Preached the Kingdom*

Matthew 9:35 And Jesus went about all the cities and villages, teaching in their synagogues, preaching the gospel of the kingdom, and healing every sickness and every disease among the people.

☞ **The preaching of the kingdom was accompanied with healing every sickness and disease among the people.**

➤ *The Kingdom Has Come*

> Luke 11:20 "But if I cast out demons with the finger of God, surely the kingdom of God has come upon you."

↪ **Jesus referred to the casting out of demons as a sign of the kingdom of God coming on us.**

➤ *The Kingdom and Disciples*

Jesus sent the twelve disciples out to preach the gospel of the kingdom.

> Matthew 10:7,8a "And as you go, preach, saying, 'The kingdom of heaven is at hand.' Heal the sick, cleanse the lepers, raise the dead, cast out demons."

↪ **The kingdom of God included healing the sick, cleansing the lepers, raising the dead and casting out demons.**

➤ *The Kingdom and Seventy*

Jesus sent the seventy to preach the gospel of the kingdom.

> Luke 10:1,9-11 After these things the Lord appointed seventy others also, and sent them two by two before His face into every city and place where He Himself was about to go.

> "And heal the sick who are there, and say to them, 'The kingdom of God has come near to you.' But whatever city you enter, and they do not receive you, go out into its streets and say, 'The very dust of your city which clings to us we wipe off against you. Nevertheless know this, that the kingdom of God has come near you.' "

↪ **The kingdom of God comes with healing. Jesus said, "heal the sick who are there, and then say, 'The kingdom of God has come.'"**

➤ *The Kingdom and Violence*

> Matthew 11:12 "And from the days of John the Baptist until now the kingdom of heaven suffers violence, and the violent take it by force. "

↪ **The kingdom of God would suffer violence, and needs to be taken by force by believers.**

➤ *Sign of the End Time*

> Matthew 24:14 "And this gospel of the kingdom will be preached in all the world as a witness to all the nations, and then the end will come."

↪ **The kingdom of God will be preached in all the world as a witness and then the end will come.**

Philip Preached the Kingdom

Philip preached the kingdom with power. The multitude heard and saw the miracles he did – the demons cried out, the paralyzed and lame were healed.

> Acts 8:5-8,12 Then Philip went down to the city of Samaria and preached Christ to them.

> And the multitudes with one accord heeded the things spoken by Philip, hearing and seeing the miracles which he did. For unclean spirits, crying with

a loud voice, came out of many who were possessed; and many who were paralyzed and lame were healed. And there was great joy in that city.

But when they believed Philip as he preached the things concerning the kingdom of God and the name of Jesus Christ, both men and women were baptized.

➪ **The first evangelistic outreach after the death and resurrection of Jesus, concerned the kingdom of God.**

Future Prophecy of the Kingdom

Revelation 11:15 Then the seventh angel sounded: And there were loud voices in heaven, saying, "The kingdoms of this world have become the kingdoms of our Lord and of His Christ, and He shall reign forever and ever!"

➪ **The kingdoms of this world will become the kingdoms of our Lord and of His anointing!**

The Kingdom Is Unshakable

Hebrews 12:25-28 See that you do not refuse Him who speaks. For if they did not escape who refused Him who spoke on earth, much more shall we not escape if we turn away from Him who speaks from heaven, whose voice then shook the earth; but now He has promised, saying, "Yet once more I shake not only the earth, but also heaven."

Now this, "Yet once more," indicates the removal of those things that are being shaken, as of things that are made, that the things which cannot be shaken may remain.

Therefore, since we are receiving a kingdom which cannot be shaken, let us have grace, by which we may serve God acceptably with reverence and godly fear.

A belief in God which is based on our own human knowledge can be shaken. A belief in God which is based on experiencing, hearing and seeing the kingdom of God preached with power, signs, wonders, and miracles, cannot be shaken. We need to pray just as Jesus said,

**"Your kingdom come.
Your will be done on earth as it is in heaven."**

THE KINGDOM IS WITHIN

We have been studying the external signs of the kingdom of God, and they are exciting! These signs are what God uses to reach the unsaved with the message of salvation. The kingdom of God is also internal – within the believer.

➢ Cannot Be Seen

Jesus said the kingdom of God could not be seen, but rather that it was of the Spirit and within us.

Luke 17:20,21 Now when He was asked by the Pharisees when the kingdom of God would come, He answered them and said, "The kingdom of God does not come with observation; nor will they say, 'See here!' or 'See there!' For indeed, the kingdom of God is within you."

Entering the Kingdom

Nicodemus came to Jesus at night.

John 3:1-4 There was a man of the Pharisees named Nicodemus, a ruler of the Jews. This man came to Jesus by night and said to Him, "Rabbi, we know that You are a teacher come from God; for no one can do these signs that You do unless God is with him."

Jesus answered and said to him, "Most assuredly, I say to you, unless one is born again, he cannot see the kingdom of God."

Nicodemus said to Him, "How can a man be born when he is old? Can he enter a second time into his mother's womb and be born?"

➤ *You Must Be Born Again*

James 3:5-7 Jesus answered, "Most assuredly, I say to you, unless one is born of water and the Spirit, he cannot enter the kingdom of God. That which is born of the flesh is flesh, and that which is born of the Spirit is spirit. Do not marvel that I said to you, 'You must be born again.'"

To be part of the kingdom of God, we must be born again – born of the Spirit. Many have prayed an intellectual prayer acknowledging they believe that Jesus is the Son of God and that He died for their sins, but they haven't entered into the spirit realm. They have made a mental decision for Christ, but they haven't been converted by a life-transforming encounter with Jesus Christ. They have not been born again by the Spirit of God. Jesus said that which is born of the flesh is flesh and that which is born of the Spirit is spirit.

The apostle Paul wrote,
1 Corinthians 2:12,14 Now we have received, not the spirit of the world, but the Spirit who is from God, that we might know the things that have been freely given to us by God.

But the natural man does not receive the things of the Spirit of God, for they are foolishness to him; nor can he know them, because they are spiritually discerned.

It's a sad fact that many who are in the churches on Sunday morning, have never actually been born again. Some have been raised in Christian homes, and know, intellectually, how to talk and act like a Christian, but they have never had a born again experience. Others, have joined an organization but never had a personal encounter with Jesus. They are good, often great, people. They may be leaders in the church, but they have never prayed accepting Jesus as their personal Savior – a prayer something like this:

From the revelation of God's Word, I realize I am a sinner. I believe that Jesus, God's only Son, was conceived by the Holy Spirit and born of the Virgin Mary. I believe He lived a sinless life and willingly died on my behalf to pay the penalty of my sin. I believe He rose from the dead and is alive today offering me the free gift of forgiveness and salvation.

I know I need to be born again. Jesus, I repent of my sins. I ask You to come into my heart and save me. I receive You as my personal Savior. Thank You Jesus, for saving me now!

It's impossible to live the Christian life, when a person doesn't have the life of God within him or herself!

If the above paragraphs have caused any doubt in your mind, pray right now. You can know you are born again. You can know you are part of the kingdom of God.

Paul wrote in Romans,
Romans 8:16 The Spirit Himself bears witness with our spirit that we are children of God.

We cannot enter into a life of prayer until we have prayed the sinner's prayer – until we have come into a right relationship with Him – until we have entered the kingdom of God.

Kingdom of God

In Romans we learn that the kingdom of God is righteousness, peace and joy in the Holy Spirit. It's not of the flesh, it's of the Spirit.

Romans 14:17 for the kingdom of God is not food and drink, but righteousness and peace and joy in the Holy Spirit.

➤ Righteousness

The kingdom of God within us is righteousness. This righteousness cannot refer to our personal righteousness because Isaiah tells us that our righteousness is as filthy rags.

Isaiah 64:6a But we are all like an unclean thing, and all our righteousnesses are like filthy rags ...

At the moment of salvation, God's righteousness is imputed to us – credited to our account. Jesus took our sins that we might have His righteousness. The kingdom of God that we are to seek is His righteousness.

Matthew 6:33a But seek first the kingdom of God and His righteousness ...

Righteousness isn't just the absence of sin, it's the positive attributes of God in all of His absolute perfect holiness and righteousness. When we pray, "Your kingdom come" as we are commanded to do, we are saying "Righteousness come."

Do we desire to be righteous? Do we desire to be holy?

As we look around the churches, we see that the divorce rate is almost as high in the church as it is in the world. Christian leaders have been caught in adultery. People who say they desire to know God are living in open rebellion against the Word of God.

We need a revelation of holiness and righteousness. We need a revelation of integrity. The apostle Peter makes it so simple. He wrote, "Be holy!"

1 Peter 1:15,16 but as He who called you is holy, you also be holy in all your conduct, because it is written, "Be holy, for I am holy."

God wants us to be righteous. We're not talking about a legalistic list of external "Do and Don'ts." True righteousness is being conformed to His image – being changed from glory to glory – being changed from the inside out!

2 Corinthians 3:18 But we all, with unveiled face, beholding as in a mirror the glory of the Lord, are being transformed into the same image from glory to glory, just as by the Spirit of the Lord.

➢ *Peace*

The kingdom of God is righteousness, peace and joy in the Holy Spirit. There's something very special about righteousness. When we seek the kingdom of God and His righteousness, suddenly there is peace – it's a normal fruit of the Holy Spirit in our lives. Peace is not something we can strive for. It's not something that is done once and for all. It's progressive.

Many think they will have peace when they have a certain amount of money in the bank. They will have peace when God straightens out their kids, or their spouse. Maybe peace will come when they get a new position, retire, or move across the country. But none of these things can bring peace.

Jesus is the Prince of Peace. When we make Him Lord of our lives – our Prince – we will have peace. Paul encourages us to let the peace of God that passes all understanding guard our hearts and minds.

Philippians 4:6,7 Be anxious for nothing, but in everything by prayer and supplication, with thanksgiving, let your requests be made known to God; and the peace of God, which surpasses all understanding, will guard your hearts and minds through Christ Jesus.

➢ *Joy*

The kingdom of God is righteousness, peace and joy. Joy isn't the surface happiness we sometimes feel. Joy comes from deep within. David wrote in the Psalms,

Psalms 16:11 You will show me the path of life; In Your presence is fullness of joy; At Your right hand are pleasures forevermore.

True joy comes from being in the presence of God.

✦ Summary – Jesus Taught on Prayer

When Jesus began to teach the disciples on prayer in response to their request, "Teach us to pray," He didn't say we were to beg, or plead. He said, "Say." We are to say to our problems, "God's kingdom come into ... , God's will be done!" We shouldn't pray our problems and our will, but pray God's will.

Knowing the kingdom of God is within us makes praying His will easier. No longer will we make up answers to our problems and ask God to fill our "shopping list." We will be so in tune with the Holy Spirit, and speaking His will on to earth, that our needs will be taken care of. We'll have a oneness in our relationship with God and be concerned with everything that concerns Him. In turn, He'll be concerned with everything that concerns us.

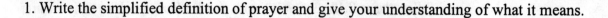

Matthew 6:33 will be in operation in our life – we will seek first the kingdom and all these things will be added to us.

QUESTIONS FOR REVIEW

1. Write the simplified definition of prayer and give your understanding of what it means.

2. Name three external signs of the kingdom of God.

3. Name three internal aspects of the kingdom of God.

4. Explain how prayer is related to the kingdom of God.

Lesson Five

Praying Brings Results

Our desire is to pray with more results. From the quick prayers we pray when we are in danger, to praying for our loved ones, to praying for the social/political situations around us, we all desire to know how to pray more effectively.

Jesus' teachings on prayer throughout the Gospels will revolutionize our prayer life.

PERSISTENCE – PERSISTENCE – PERSISTENCE

Some prayers aren't answered because they were never prayed. Sometimes, we talk about a situation, mention we are going to pray about it, but never get around to actually doing it. Other times prayers aren't answered because we didn't persist in prayer.

The apostle Paul wrote,
Ephesians 6:18 ... praying always with all prayer and supplication in the Spirit, being watchful to this end with all perseverance and supplication for all the saints.

Isaiah set watchmen on the wall who would never hold their peace. They would not keep silent but would pray continuously.

Isaiah 62:6,7 I have set watchmen on your walls, O Jerusalem, who shall never hold their peace day or night. You who make mention of the LORD, do not keep silent, and give Him no rest till He establishes and till He makes Jerusalem a praise in the earth.

Jesus Taught Persistence

Jesus taught us to be persistent in praying.

Luke 11:5-8 And He said to them, "Which of you shall have a friend, and go to him at midnight and say to him, 'Friend, lend me three loaves; for a friend of mine has come to me on his journey, and I have nothing to set before him'; and he will answer from within and say, 'Do not trouble me; the door is now shut, and my children are with me in bed; I cannot rise and give to you'?

"I say to you, though he will not rise and give to him because he is his friend, yet because of his persistence he will rise and give him as many as he needs."

Pray Day and Night

He said we should pray day and night and not lose heart.

Luke 18:1,7,8a Then He spoke a parable to them, that men always ought to pray and not lose heart.

"And shall God not avenge His own elect who cry out day and night to Him though He bears long with them? I tell you that He will avenge them speedily."

Three Steps of Prayer

Jesus also gave us three steps to a successful prayer life: ask – seek – and knock.

Matthew 7:7-11 "Ask, and it will be given to you; seek, and you will find; knock, and it will be opened to you. For everyone who asks receives, and he who seeks finds, and to him who knocks it will be opened.

"Or what man is there among you who, if his son asks for bread, will give him a stone? Or if he asks for a fish, will he give him a serpent?

"If you then, being evil, know how to give good gifts to your children, how much more will your Father who is in heaven give good things to those who ask Him!"

➤ *Ask and Receive*

Ask implies a dependence on God, a coming to Him with our requests. We are to ask just as the blind men sitting near the road called, "Lord that our eyes may be opened!" When we ask in faith, we will be expecting to receive.

Jesus promised us that if we ask, we will receive.

➤ *Seek and Find*

Seek speaks of purposeful enterprise, of an urgency constraining us to search until we find. This might best be typified by the woman with an issue of blood pushing her way through the crowd saying, "The moment I touch Him, I shall be healed."

No one seeks for something unless they expect to find it – unless they are desperate to find it.

When we ask for something we feel is God's will for our lives, and the answer doesn't seem to come, we should seek for it. This would include seeking for more of God's Word on the subject. It would also include seeking out problem areas that may be in our lives preventing our answer from being manifested.

Jesus promised us that if we seek, we will find.

➤ *Knock and It Will Open*

Knock carries the idea of being persistent, of having an unwillingness to let go until we receive. The Syro-Phoenician woman is the best example of this.

Mark 7:25-30 For a woman whose young daughter had an unclean spirit heard about Him, and she came and fell at His feet. The woman was a Greek, a Syro-Phoenician by birth, and she kept asking Him to cast the demon out of her daughter.

But Jesus said to her, "Let the children be filled first, for it is not good to take the children's bread and throw it to the little dogs."

And she answered and said to Him, "Yes, Lord, yet even the little dogs under the table eat from the children's crumbs."

Then He said to her, "For this saying go your way; the demon has gone out of your daughter." And when she had come to her house, she found the demon gone out, and her daughter lying on the bed.

Knock means to be persistent, to "push into God," to quote the Word of God until it moves from our understanding to our spirit.

Again, Jesus said that when we knock it would be opened.

We must not give up on the brink of our miracle. We must persist in prayer and faith until the answer comes. We must do as Jesus said, ask in faith expecting to receive – seek expecting to find – knock on doors expecting them to open.

PRAY IN SECRET

Don't Pray to Be Seen

Have you ever listened to someone talking about their prayer life and inside you didn't feel right? They might have been saying, "I pray for at least an hour every morning." "I do this" or "I do that." That's great! But why are they telling others. What is their motive?

Sometimes a person will pray a beautiful prayer, but they are praying for the benefit of those listening instead of going humbly before God.

We don't need to know the motives of others but we are to judge our own. It's only God Who knows the real motives of a person's heart.

1 Samuel 16:7b ... for man looks at the outward appearance, but the LORD looks at the heart.

Jesus talked about the prayers of the hypocrites.

Matthew 6:5 "And when you pray, you shall not be like the hypocrites. For they love to pray standing in the synagogues and on the corners of the streets, that they may be seen by men. Assuredly, I say to you, they have their reward."

Jesus told us to pray secretly. Perhaps, at least partially, to keep our prayers from becoming tainted with the admiration or criticism of those around us.

➤ *Shut the Door*

Matthew 6:6 "But you, when you pray, go into your room, and when you have shut your door, pray to your Father who is in the secret place; and your Father who sees in secret will reward you openly."

DO NOT USE VAIN REPETITIONS

Matthew 6:7-8a "But when you pray, do not use vain repetitions as the heathen do. For they think that they will be heard for their many words. Therefore do not be like them."

Vain repetitions means we aren't to chant words to God. Neither are we to pray the same thing over and over again, either for a period of time, or day after day with no faith. Vain repetitions are expressions of worry and unbelief.

Sometimes when we are in the midst of a tension filled situation, we may need something so desperately, we realize we are saying the same words over and over. At times like these, we must stop the repetition and begin to quote the Word of God. This we can do over and over, because it's by hearing and hearing the Word that faith comes into our spirits. By quoting God's promises, we will be building ourselves up so that faith can come.

Your Father Already Knows

God knows our needs before we ask. It's no surprise to Him when something comes unexpectedly into our lives. Jesus talked about this immediately after he spoke about vain repetition.

Matthew 6:8b "For your Father knows the things you have need of before you ask Him."

Elijah Opposes Baal's Priests

The strongest example of vain repetition is found in the confrontation between Elijah and the priests of Baal.

1 Kings 18:26-29 So they took the bull which was given them, and they prepared it, and called on the name of Baal from morning even till noon, saying, "O Baal, hear us!" But there was no voice; no one answered. And they leaped about the altar which they had made.

And so it was, at noon, that Elijah mocked them and said, "Cry aloud, for he is a god; either he is meditating, or he is busy, or he is on a journey, or perhaps he is sleeping and must be awakened."

So they cried aloud, and cut themselves, as was their custom, with knives and lances, until the blood gushed out on them. And it was so, when midday was past, that they prophesied until the time of the offering of the evening sacrifice. But there was no voice; no one answered, no one paid attention.

The priests of Baal had leaped about the altar, and cried out all day. They had cut themselves until their blood gushed out, but there was no Baal to answer.

Elijah approached God in the opposite way. He rebuilt the altar of the Lord, and had them pour water over the sacrifice until the sacrifice was soaked. Then Elijah came near and *said* – he didn't scream, or leap, or beat himself. These are all signs of unbelief. He said ... and the sacrifice was consumed.

1 Kings 18:30-39 Then Elijah said to all the people, "Come near to me." So all the people came near to him. And he repaired the altar of the LORD that was broken down. Then with the stones he built an altar in the name of the LORD; and he made a trench around the altar large enough to hold two seahs of seed. And he put the wood in order, cut the bull in pieces, and laid it on the wood, and said, "Fill four waterpots with water, and pour it on the burnt sacrifice and on the wood."

Then he said, "Do it a second time," and they did it a second time; and he said, "Do it a third time," and they did it a third time. So the water ran all around the altar; and he also filled the trench with water.

➤ *His Prayer*

And it came to pass, at the time of the offering of the evening sacrifice, that Elijah the prophet came near and said, "LORD God of Abraham, Isaac, and Israel, let it be known this day that You are God in Israel, and that I am Your servant, and that I have done all these things at Your word. Hear me, O LORD, hear me, that this people may know that You are the LORD God, and that You have turned their hearts back to You again."

Then the fire of the LORD fell and consumed the burnt sacrifice, and the wood and the stones and the dust, and it licked up the water that was in the trench.

Now when all the people saw it, they fell on their faces; and they said, "The LORD, He is God! The LORD, He is God!"

REMOVE THE HINDRANCES

When Jesus taught on prayer, He taught about those things that would prevent our prayers from being heard.

The reason Jesus could pray – could speak – and it was done instantly, wasn't because He was the Son of God. He operated on this earth as the Last Adam. He operated as Adam and Eve had been created to act. The reason His prayers were answered so powerfully was because of the absolute purity of His life. There were no hindrances.

Too many times, we allow ourselves to be involved in situations of mixture, even of sin, and then wonder why God doesn't answer our prayers.

The apostle Paul warned us,
Galatians 6:7,8 Do not be deceived, God is not mocked; for whatever a man sows, that he will also reap. For he who sows to his flesh will of the flesh reap corruption, but he who sows to the Spirit will of the Spirit reap everlasting life.

To become more powerful men and women of prayer, we must take time to understand and remove every hindrance.

Unbelief

When Jesus returned to His own country, even though He had perfect faith, He did no mighty works there. Matthew tells us the reason was unbelief. Unbelief is the total opposite of faith.

Matthew 13:54-58 And when He had come to His own country, He taught them in their synagogue, so that they were astonished and said, "Where did this Man get this wisdom and these mighty works? Is this not the carpenter's son? Is not His mother called Mary? And His brothers James, Joses, Simon, and Judas? And His sisters, are they not all with us? Where then did this Man get all these things?" So they were offended at Him.

But Jesus said to them, "A prophet is not without honor except in his own country and in his own house." And He did not do many mighty works there because of their unbelief.

What did Jesus say to the ruler of the synagogue when the word came to him, "Your daughter is dead?" "Only Believe."

What did Jesus say to the blind men begging beside the road? "According to your faith."

What did Jesus say to Martha at the tomb of Lazarus? "If you would believe you would see the glory of God!"

We cannot receive answers to our prayers if we are living in doubt and unbelief.

James 1:5-7 If any of you lacks wisdom, let him ask of God, who gives to all liberally and without reproach, and it will be given to him. But let him ask in faith, with no doubting, for he who doubts is like a wave of the sea driven and tossed by the wind. For let not that man suppose that he will receive anything from the Lord.

Lack of Knowledge

In the books of Isaiah and Hosea, we read some very challenging statements.

Isaiah 5:13a Therefore my people have gone into captivity, because they have no knowledge ...

Hosea 4:6a My people are destroyed for lack of knowledge.

If we don't know what the Word of God says about a situation, how can we have faith? True faith can only be based on the Word of God.

Knowledge is based on knowing God and His righteousness.

Romans 10:2,3 For I bear them witness that they have a zeal for God, but not according to knowledge. For they being ignorant of God's righteousness, and seeking to establish their own righteousness, have not submitted to the righteousness of God.

Pride and Pretense

Jesus contrasted the prayer of the proud with that of the humble.

Luke 18:9b-14 "Two men went up to the temple to pray, one a Pharisee and the other a tax collector. The Pharisee stood and prayed thus with himself, 'God, I thank You that I am not like other men – extortioners, unjust, adulterers, or even as this tax collector. I fast twice a week; I give tithes of all that I possess.'

"And the tax collector, standing afar off, would not so much as raise his eyes to heaven, but beat his breast, saying, 'God be merciful to me a sinner!'"

"I tell you, this man went down to his house justified rather than the other; for everyone who exalts himself will be abased, and he who humbles himself will be exalted."

Jesus called the scribes and Pharisees hypocrites because they prayed prayers of pretense.

Matthew 23:14 "Woe to you, scribes and Pharisees, hypocrites! For you devour widows' houses, and for a pretense make long prayers. Therefore you will receive greater condemnation."

Unforgiveness

We live in a very imperfect world. All of us have been, to some degree, hurt, abused, rejected, and lied about. How often we have heard someone say, "But they don't deserve to be forgiven." Actually, what the person deserves has nothing to do with forgiveness. God never made our need to forgive conditional on what the other person does, or doesn't do. That would position them to still be in control of us.

It's not that God is trying to make it easier on the other person or persons. God's desire is to make it easier on us. As long as we hold on to unforgiveness, we cannot go on to a better life ourselves. Unforgiveness holds us in bondage to that person or situation. The only way their hold over us can be broken is for us to forgive them.

➢ *Forgive to Be Forgiven*

Jesus taught that our prayers cannot be answered as long as there is unforgiveness in our hearts.

Mark 11:25-26 "And whenever you stand praying, if you have anything against anyone, forgive him, that your Father in heaven may also forgive you your trespasses. But if you do not forgive, neither will your Father in heaven forgive your trespasses."

The opposite thought to our forgiving others is asking others to forgive us. Notice, Jesus didn't say if we have wronged our brother (or sister in the Lord). He said if they have something against us.

Matthew 5:23,24 "Therefore if you bring your gift to the altar, and there remember that your brother has something against you, leave your gift there before the altar, and go your way. First be reconciled to your brother, and then come and offer your gift."

Jesus made forgiveness part of the Lord's Prayer and He taught more on forgiving immediately following that prayer. He couldn't have been more clear – if you want God to forgive you, forgive others.

Matthew 6:12,14,15 "And forgive us our debts, As we forgive our debtors ... For if you forgive men their trespasses, your heavenly Father will also forgive you. But if you do not forgive men their trespasses, neither will your Father forgive your trespasses."

➢ *Seven Times Seventy*

Peter had grown up under a system of laws. His question to Jesus was, "Is it enough to forgive seven times?" He was asking for a religious rule.

Matthew 18:21,22 Then Peter came to Him and said, "Lord, how often shall my brother sin against me, and I forgive him? Up to seven times?"

Jesus said to him, "I do not say to you, up to seven times, but up to seventy times seven."

Jesus' reply of "seventy times seven" was an indication that they were to develop a continuous life-style of forgiving. It would be impossible to keep track of the times we forgive someone up to four hundred and ninety times.

➢ *The Wicked Servant*

Jesus told a parable about the importance of forgiving.

Matthew 18:23-35 "Therefore the kingdom of heaven is like a certain king who wanted to settle accounts with his servants. And when he had begun to settle accounts, one was brought to him who owed him ten thousand talents. But as he was not able to pay, his master commanded that he be sold, with his wife and children and all that he had, and that payment be made. The servant therefore fell down before him, saying, 'Master, have patience with me, and I will pay you all.'

"Then the master of that servant was moved with compassion, released him, and forgave him the debt. But that servant went out and found one of his fellow servants who owed him a hundred denarii; and he laid hands on him and took him by the throat, saying, 'Pay me what you owe!'

"So his fellow servant fell down at his feet and begged him, saying, 'Have patience with me, and I will pay you all.' And he would not, but went and threw him into prison till he should pay the debt. So when his fellow servants saw what had been done, they were very grieved, and came and told their master all that had been done.

"Then his master, after he had called him, said to him, 'You wicked servant! I forgave you all that debt because you begged me. Should you not also have had compassion on your fellow servant, just as I had pity on you?' And his master was angry, and delivered him to the torturers until he should pay all that was due to him.

"So My heavenly Father also will do to you if each of you, from his heart, does not forgive his brother his trespasses."

We have been forgiven of so much by God – our sins of the past and our failures in the present – how can we not forgive others?

REMOVE THE BARRIER OF SIN

From the time Adam and Eve hid themselves from God in the Garden of Eden, sin has stood as a barrier between a holy God and sinful men and women.

Isaiah 59:1,2 Behold, the Lord's hand is not shortened, that it cannot save; nor His ear heavy, that it cannot hear. But your iniquities have separated you from your God; and your sins have hidden His face from you, so that He will not hear.

Jesus has paid the penalty for our sin, but we must take advantage of His provision for the forgiveness and removal of sin. Many books have been written on prayer with the presumption that these facts are self-evident. But men and women have a tremendous ability to convince themselves that sin, theirs in particular, is understood and overlooked by God. This is not so. Solomon wrote,

Proverbs 14:12 There is a way which seems right to a man, but its end is the way of death.

God cannot overlook sin. It's contrary to His nature and to His Word. A holy God cannot be in the presence of sin, and His grace isn't an automatic overlooking or forgiveness of sin.

Romans 6:1,2 What shall we say then? Shall we continue in sin that grace may abound? Certainly not! How shall we who died to sin live any longer in it?

Sin in our life in any form will stop our prayers from being heard.

Confess and Be Forgiven

How do we get rid of sin in our lives? By being honest with ourselves and God, by calling sin what it is, and confessing it to God. We cannot make excuses. "Well, I didn't mean it that way, but ..." We cannot say, "It's just a little thing ..."

To be forgiven and cleansed of unrighteousness, we must face our sin honestly and confess it to God.

1 John 1:9 If we confess our sins, He is faithful and just to forgive us our sins and to cleanse us from all unrighteousness.

If our prayers aren't answered, we should take time to discover the reasons. It may not be sin, but rather from a lack of knowledge, a lack of faith, or from not asking according to God's will.

Barriers to Answered Prayer

➤ *Iniquities*

Iniquities are the sins that have been passed down from generation to generation.

Jeremiah 11:10,11 "They have turned back to the iniquities of their forefathers who refused to hear My words, and they have gone after other gods to serve them; the house of Israel and the house of Judah have broken My covenant which I made with their fathers." Therefore thus says the LORD: "Behold, I will surely bring calamity on them which they will not be able to escape; and though they cry out to Me, I will not listen to them."

David wrote,
Psalms 66:18 If I regard iniquity in my heart, The Lord will not hear.

➤ *Having Idols in the Heart*

Anything in our lives, which is put in the place of the importance that God should have, becomes an idol. God must have first place in our lives.

Ezekiel 14:3 Son of man, these men have set up their idols in their hearts, and put before them that which causes them to stumble into iniquity. Should I let Myself be inquired of at all by them?

➤ *Stealing, Murder, Committing Adultery*
Swearing Falsely, Serving other Gods

Jeremiah 7:9,10,13,16 "Will you steal, murder, commit adultery, swear falsely, burn incense to Baal, and walk after other gods whom you do not know, and then come and stand before Me in this house which is called by My name, and say, `We are delivered to do all these abominations'?"

"And now, because you have done all these works," says the LORD, "and I spoke to you, rising up early and speaking, but you did not hear, and I called you, but you did not answer."

"Therefore [Jeremiah] do not pray for this people, nor lift up a cry or prayer for them, nor make intercession to Me; for I will not hear you."

What did God say to Jeremiah? Don't make intercession, or cry, or pray for them, for I will not hear you.

"Them" refers to those who steal, murder, commit adultery, swear falsely, serve other gods, and then come to God's house and say, "We are delivered to do these things." Could this be the same as saying, "We're under grace, not the law. We can sin and God will forgive us?" Could this be the same as saying, "I know the Bible says ... is wrong, but God understands my situation?"

➤ *Being Proud*

God will not hear the proud.

Job 35:12,13 There they cry out, but He does not answer, because of the pride of evil men. Surely God will not listen to empty talk, nor will the Almighty regard it.

James 4:6b "God resists the proud, but gives grace to the humble."

➤ *Being Unhearing*

God will not hear those who shut their ears to the poor.

Proverbs 21:13 Whoever shuts his ears to the cry of the poor will also cry himself and not be heard.

➤ *Being Disobedient*

Disobedience to God's Word is very serious. Isaiah said it was as the sin of witchcraft. God will not listen to the disobedient.

1 Samuel 15:23a For rebellion is as the sin of witchcraft, and stubbornness is as iniquity and idolatry.

Zechariah 7:11-13 "But they refused to heed, shrugged their shoulders, and stopped their ears so that they could not hear. Yes, they made their hearts like flint, refusing to hear the law and the words which the LORD of hosts had sent by His Spirit through the former prophets. Thus great wrath came from the LORD of hosts."

"Therefore it happened, that just as He proclaimed and they would not hear, so they called out and I would not listen," says the LORD of hosts.

Proverbs 28:9 One who turns away his ear from hearing the law, even his prayer shall be an abomination.

➤ *Dishonoring Wife*

The relationship between a husband and wife is to be an earthly picture of the relationship between Jesus and the church – the body of Christ. Peter spoke about this relationship not being right and our prayers being hindered.

1 Peter 3:7 Likewise you husbands, dwell with them with understanding, giving honor to the wife, as to the weaker vessel, and as being heirs together of the grace of life, that your prayers may not be hindered.

In Conclusion

If there is anything which our conscience reproves us for, we will not be able to pray with confidence until it's forgiven. A pure conscience and faith are linked together and cannot be separated.

1 Timothy 1:5 Now the purpose of the commandment is love from a pure heart, from a good conscience, and from sincere faith.

BE ENCOURAGED TO PRAY

Jesus Said Pray

Jesus commanded us to pray and encouraged us to pray continually.

Matthew 9:38 "Therefore pray the Lord of the harvest to send out laborers into His harvest."

Luke 18:1 Then He spoke a parable to them, that men always ought to pray and not lose heart.

Luke 21:36 "Watch therefore, and pray always that you may be counted worthy to escape all these things that will come to pass, and to stand before the Son of Man."

Apostles Encouraged Prayer

The first deacons were put into position in the church so that the apostles could give themselves to prayer and the ministry of the Word.

Acts 6:4 "but we will give ourselves continually to prayer and to the ministry of the word."

The apostle Paul said it was his desire that we pray always in holiness, without anger or doubting.

1 Timothy 2:8 Therefore I desire that the men pray everywhere, lifting up holy hands, without wrath and doubting.

Ephesians 6:18 Praying always with all prayer and supplication in the Spirit, being watchful to this end with all perseverance and supplication for all the saints.

James said we are to pray for one another.

James 5:16 Confess your trespasses to one another, and pray for one another, that you may be healed. The effective, fervent prayer of a righteous man avails much.

Peter told us to be serious and watchful in prayer.

1 Peter 4:7 But the end of all things is at hand; therefore be serious and watchful in your prayers.

David Prayed

The book of Psalms is full of David's prayers. He said he gave himself to prayer.

Psalms 109:4b But I give myself to prayer.

Prayer Glorifies God

Jesus said,
John 14:13 "And whatever you ask in My name, that I will do, that the Father may be glorified in the Son."

Prayer Delights God

Proverbs 15:8 The sacrifice of the wicked is an abomination to the LORD, but the prayer of the upright is His delight.

God Hears and Answers Prayers

Psalms 65:2 O You who hear prayer, To You all flesh will come.

Psalms 86:7 In the day of my trouble I will call upon You, For You will answer me.

1 Peter 3:12a For the eyes of the Lord are on the righteous, and his ears are open to their prayers.

✦ Summary – Praying Brings Results

Jesus said we are to be persistent in prayer. We are to pray day and night. We are to ask, seek and knock in prayer. He also said we must not pray to be seen, but should rather pray in private. We are not to pray the same thing over and over, because that is not praying in faith, since God already knows our needs.

Jesus made it clear that if we are not walking in forgiveness toward others, we are not to pray until we go and make it right. We are to forgive those who have hurt us and we are to ask forgiveness of those we have hurt or who have negative feelings toward us.

Unbelief, lack of knowledge, pride, iniquity, stealing, murder, committing adultery, swearing falsely, and serving other gods – all sin – will all cause our prayers to go unanswered.

When we come to God in prayer, we should first remove anything that keeps us from coming freely into His presence. Then our prayers can be prayed in faith.

QUESTIONS FOR REVIEW

1. List and explain three steps to praying effectively.

3. How can we know if there are any barriers or hindrances in our life that are preventing God from answering our prayers?

2. Name any barriers or hindrances to prayer that have been a problem in your life. What do you plan to do about them?

Lesson Six

Entering a Successful Prayer Life

INTRODUCTION

We were raised in churches where the emphasis was to study the Word. We heard Paul's admonition to Timothy many times.

2 Timothy 2:15 (KJV) Study to shew thyself approved unto God, a workman that needeth not to be ashamed, rightly dividing the word of truth.

We studied to gain God's approval, and we thank God for everything we learned during those years. But we didn't know that true study shouldn't only be dedicated to learning with our natural mind, but also allowing the Holy Spirit to be our Teacher – of being dependent on His revelation.

➢ *The Bones*

The knowledge of the Word can be compared to the bone structure of the body. It allows us to live and move with purpose. Without it we would be like jellyfish waiting for the waves to carry us here or there.

There is another verse we never heard emphasized. When we learn something, we are to put it into practice. We are to do it! The apostle James said we were not to be hearers only of the Word. We were to be doers of the Word.

James 1:22-24 But be doers of the word, and not hearers only, deceiving yourselves. For if anyone is a hearer of the word and not a doer, he is like a man observing his natural face in a mirror; for he observes himself, goes away, and immediately forgets what kind of man he was.

➢ *The Flesh*

To carry the analogy of the body further, the will and emotions are like the flesh and blood. Love, joy, peace, longsuffering, kindness, goodness, faithfulness, gentleness, self-control are all in this area.

➢ *The Spirit*

There is still another part of a living body and that is the human spirit. Prayer is an expression of worship, and we are to worship in the spirit.

John 4:23,24 "But the hour is coming, and now is, when the true worshipers will worship the Father in spirit and truth; for the Father is seeking such to worship Him. God is Spirit, and those who worship Him must worship in spirit and truth."

HOW DO WE PRAY

It's not enough to study about prayer, we must do it. We are to pray to God the Father, through His Son, in the power of the Holy Spirit.

To God – The Father

➤ *Jesus Our Example*

Jesus prayed to God as Father.

John 17:1 Jesus spoke these words, lifted up His eyes to heaven, and said: "Father, the hour has come. Glorify Your Son, that Your Son also may glorify You."

He referred to God as Holy Father.

John 17:11 "Now I am no longer in the world, but these are in the world, and I come to You. Holy Father, keep through Your name those whom You have given Me, that they may be one as We are."

He referred to God as Righteous Father.

John 17:25 "O righteous Father! The world has not known You, but I have known You; and these have known that You sent Me."

Jesus said we were to address God as our Father in heaven.

Matthew 6:9 "In this manner, therefore, pray: Our Father in heaven, hallowed be Your name."

➤ *Others Prayed to Jesus*

Although we are instructed and encouraged to pray to God the Father, this isn't a legalistic rule that must be followed at all times. We know this because Stephen, at the moment of death, prayed to Jesus.

Acts 7:59 And they stoned Stephen as he was calling on God and saying, "Lord Jesus, receive my spirit."

There are people who have been so hurt by their earthly fathers that they are afraid to pray to their heavenly Father. God understands this. As their relationship with Jesus grows, He will reveal the true, loving heavenly Father to them and bring them into relationship with Him.

In the Name of Jesus

We are to pray to God in the name of Jesus. Our position before God is in Jesus. We are justified in Him.

John 15:16 "You did not choose Me, but I chose you and appointed you that ... whatever you ask the Father in My name He may give you."

Through the Holy Spirit

There is no instance in the Bible of a prayer to the Holy Spirit. However, prayer should be through the Holy Spirit, in dependence on Him.

Romans 8:26 Likewise the Spirit also helps in our weaknesses. For we do not know what we should pray for as we ought, but the Spirit Himself makes intercession for us with groanings which cannot be uttered.

The apostle Paul said we have access to God the Father through Jesus and by the Holy Spirit.

Ephesians 2:18 For through Him we both have access by one Spirit to the Father.

APPROACHING GOD WITH RIGHT ATTITUDES

Repentance

In the Lord's Prayer, Jesus taught us to pray, "Forgive us our sins." This should always be part of our prayer life.

➤ *David*

King David sinned and when confronted with that sin, he became an example of repentance for us.

Psalms 51:1 Have mercy upon me, O God, According to Your lovingkindness; According to the multitude of Your tender mercies, Blot out my transgressions.

➤ *Prodigal Son*

One of the most beautiful stories of repentance is that of the Prodigal Son. He had rebelled against his father and gone his own way. Finally at the point of starving, he decided to return to his father and ask for his forgiveness. He did just that. When the father met him with outstretched arms of love, he didn't say to himself, "O, I guess he doesn't see me as bad as I am. I can just forget being so humble. My father understands ..." If we get away from God, we are to come humbly to Him asking for forgiveness.

Luke 15:18-23 'I will arise and go to my father, and will say to him, "Father, I have sinned against heaven and before you, and I am no longer worthy to be called your son. Make me like one of your hired servants." ' And he arose and came to his father.

"But when he was still a great way off, his father saw him and had compassion, and ran and fell on his neck and kissed him.

"And the son said to him, 'Father, I have sinned against heaven and in your sight, and am no longer worthy to be called your son.'

"But the father said to his servants, 'Bring out the best robe and put it on him, and put a ring on his hand and sandals on his feet. And bring the fatted calf here and kill it, and let us eat and be merry ...' "

Our heavenly Father meets us with open arms when we simply come to Him and say, "I have sinned."

Humility

Humility means to show a deferential, or submissive, respect to God. It means to submit to the opinion, wishes, and decision of God through respect, in recognition of His authority, knowledge, and judgment, and to know we are coming in His name – not in our own knowledge, position, or abilities.

2 Chronicles 7:14 "if My people who are called by My name will humble themselves, and pray and seek My face, and turn from their wicked ways, then I will hear from heaven, and will forgive their sin and heal their land. "

We are to humble ourselves before God in prayer.

Obedience

John made it very clear that obedience has much to do with our prayers being answered.

1 John 3:22 And whatever we ask we receive from Him, because we keep His commandments and do those things that are pleasing in His sight.

Faith

When Jesus was ministering to people, He continuously encouraged them to have faith.

Mark 11:22-24 So Jesus answered and said to them, "Have faith in God. For assuredly, I say to you, whoever says to this mountain, 'Be removed and be cast into the sea,' and does not doubt in his heart, but believes that those things he says will come to pass, he will have whatever he says. Therefore I say to you, whatever things you ask when you pray, believe that you receive them, and you will have them."

Matthew 8:13 Then Jesus said to the centurion, "Go your way; and as you have believed, so let it be done for you." And his servant was healed that same hour.

Matthew 9:28 And when He had come into the house, the blind men came to Him. And Jesus said to them, "Do you believe that I am able to do this?" They said to Him, "Yes, Lord."

Mark 5:36 As soon as Jesus heard the word that was spoken, He said to the ruler of the synagogue, "Do not be afraid; only believe."

Mark 9:23 Jesus said to him, "If you can believe, all things are possible to him who believes."

Luke 8:48 And He said to her, "Daughter, be of good cheer; your faith has made you well. Go in peace."

Without faith, it is impossible to please God.

Hebrews 11:6 But without faith it is impossible to please Him, for he who comes to God must believe that He is, and that He is a rewarder of those who diligently seek Him.

STEPS TO SUCCESS IN PRAYER

Abiding in Christ

The first step to praying successful prayers is abiding in Christ. We are to develop a life-style of being in Him. Jesus said if we do this, we can ask whatever we desire and it will be done.

John 15:7 "If you abide in Me, and My words abide in you, you will ask what you desire, and it shall be done for you."

David said that the Lord would give us the desires of our heart – if we first delight ourselves in Him. As we do this, we are

Psalms 37:4 Delight yourself also in the LORD, And He shall give you the desires of your heart. Commit your way to the LORD, Trust also in Him, And He shall bring it to pass.

Ask According to His Will

The apostle John gave us a wonderful promise that if we ask anything according to God's will, we have what we ask.

1 John 5:14,15 Now this is the confidence that we have in Him, that if we ask anything according to His will, He hears us. And if we know that He hears us, whatever we ask, we know that we have the petitions that we have asked of Him.

James wrote that we will not receive the answer to our prayers if we ask contrary to the will of God, selfishly, or with carnal motives for our own pleasures.

James 4:3 You ask and do not receive, because you ask amiss, that you may spend it on your pleasures.

At this point, the question becomes, how do we know what is according to His will? James said we were to ask God.

James 1:5 If any of you lacks wisdom, let him ask of God, who gives to all liberally and without reproach, and it will be given to him.

➤ *David Prayed God's Will*

David prayed for his house – not a physical house, but for his lineage, for his descendants. He based this prayer on what he had heard from God. He prayed according to that word.

2 Samuel 7:26-29 "So let Your name be magnified forever, saying, 'The LORD of hosts is the God over Israel.' And let the house of Your servant David be established before You. For You, O LORD of hosts, God of Israel, have revealed this to Your servant, saying, 'I will build you a house.' Therefore Your servant found it in his heart to pray this prayer to You.

"And now, O LORD God, You are God, and Your words are true, and You have promised this goodness to Your servant. Now therefore, let it please You to bless the house of Your servant, that it may continue forever before You; for You, O LORD God, have spoken it, and with Your blessing let the house of Your servant be blessed forever."

David heard God's will and he prayed it back to God confirming it in his own spirit, speaking it forth so that it could become a reality.

➤ *Elisha Raised Dead Child*

The following example of answered prayer is exciting, but so much is left unsaid.

2 Kings 4:32-35 And when Elisha came into the house, there was the child, lying dead on his bed. He went in therefore, shut the door behind the two of them, and prayed to the LORD.

And he went up and lay on the child, and put his mouth on his mouth, his eyes on his eyes, and his hands on his hands; and he stretched himself out on the child, and the flesh of the child became warm.

And he went up and lay on the child, and put his mouth on his mouth, his eyes on his eyes, and his hands on his hands; and he stretched himself out on the child, and the flesh of the child became warm.

He returned and walked back and forth in the house, and again went up and stretched himself out on him; then the child sneezed seven times, and the child opened his eyes.

Elisha heard about the need, he prayed, and then he went to the child. He must have done what God told him to do because he didn't do the natural thing. He laid on the dead child. The flesh became warm, but the miracle wasn't complete.

Then Elisha came out of the room and walked back and forth in the house. He must have been praying – perhaps confirming with the Lord what he had heard – perhaps engaging in spiritual warfare – and then he returned to the child, laid on him the second time, and the child opened his eyes.

Elisha didn't say "wouldn't it be nice if ... ," and move into action. He prayed first and then he acted on the revelation he had received.

Pray in Truth

John said the Spirit of truth will guide us and tell us.

John 16:13 "However, when He, the Spirit of truth, has come, He will guide you into all truth; for He will not speak on His own authority, but whatever He hears He will speak; and He will tell you things to come."

When we pray, we must be honest with ourselves and with God. The Hebrew word for truth also carries a meaning of stability and trustworthiness.

Psalms 145:18 The LORD is near to all who call upon Him, To all who call upon Him in truth.

Pray in the Spirit

In Lesson One, we discussed two languages of prayer – with the spirit and with the understanding. The apostle Jude wrote,

Jude 1:20 But you, beloved, building yourselves up on your most holy faith, praying in the Holy Spirit ...

The apostle Paul said in Ephesians 6:17-19 that we should be praying always with all prayer and supplication in the Spirit ... that utterance may be given to me.

We should never pray without first looking to the Holy Spirit for help.

Romans 8:26 Likewise the Spirit also helps in our weaknesses. For we do not know what we should pray for as we ought, but the Spirit Himself makes intercession for us with groanings which cannot be uttered.

When God has confirmed what He desires to do in a situation either through His Word, or through the Holy Spirit, faith comes into our spirits. We can pray with boldness and confidence.

Ephesians 3:12 In whom (Christ) we have boldness and access with confidence through faith in Him.

Pray Earnestly, Intensely

God absolutely rejects our being lukewarm. He says I wish you were either hot or cold. We must stop saying "Well, whatever you say, God. Whatever you want ..."

Revelation 3:14-16 "And to the angel of the church of the Laodiceans write, 'These things says the Amen, the Faithful and True Witness, the Beginning of the creation of God: I know your works, that you are neither cold nor hot. I could wish you were cold or hot. So then, because you are lukewarm, and neither cold nor hot, I will spew you out of My mouth.' "

We must know God, know His Word, know what He has given us and go after it. God gave the children of Israel the Promised Land, but they had to fight for it. They had to go in and possess the land.

Pray Without Ceasing

When Paul wrote the church at Thessalonica, he said they were to pray without ceasing. How is this possible? How can you and I take care of the normal responsibilities of life and pray without ceasing?

We do it by developing a life-style of prayer – by scheduling a prayer time each day, and then by allowing our spirits to continue praying throughout the day.

1 Thessalonians 5:17 pray without ceasing.

➤ *Constantly*

When Peter was thrown into prison, the other believers prayed for him constantly. They didn't say, "Well, whatever happens, you know God's in charge."

Acts 12:5 Peter was therefore kept in prison, but constant prayer was offered to God for him by the church.

➤ *Effectively, Fervently, Earnestly*

When James said we were to pray for one another, he reminded us of Elijah praying fervently.

James 5:16,17a Confess your trespasses to one another, and pray for one another, that you may be healed. The effective, fervent prayer of a righteous man avails much. Elijah was a man with a nature like ours, and he prayed earnestly ...

➤ *Laboring*

Paul labored fervently in prayer. Surely, with his great ministry, and with the books he wrote, he didn't find it easy to take time for prayer, and yet he wrote these words – "always laboring fervently for you in prayers."

Colossians 4:12 Epaphras, who is one of you, a servant of Christ, greets you, always laboring fervently for you in prayers, that you may stand perfect and complete in all the will of God.

➢ Striving

Paul used the word "strive." It means to exert much effort, energy, or endeavor; to struggle or fight forcefully; to contend. Paul didn't want any lukewarm, "maybe if it's your will" prayers. Paul was in a battle and he begged the brethren to strive with him in prayer.

Romans 15:30 Now I beg you, brethren, through the Lord Jesus Christ, and through the love of the Spirit, that you strive together with me in your prayers to God for me.

➢ Travailing

Travailing is a word used much more in the King James Version of the Bible, than in the newer translations. The word translated travail, in cases other than a woman giving birth, means to toil, to work long and hard. The apostle Paul wrote to the believers in Galatia that he was travailing in prayer until Christ be formed in them. This is the only verse that has the meaning of prayer as travailing as in birth for another and it was written of believers.

Galatians 4:19 [KJV] My little children, of whom I travail in birth again until Christ be formed in you.

Once birth pangs have started, they continue until the baby is born. Travailing in prayer carries a meaning of continuing on with great intensity until the battle has been won in the spirit.

➢ Seeking

We are to seek God with our whole heart. Moses prophesied over his people that they would seek with all their hearts.

Deuteronomy 4:29 "But from there you will seek the LORD your God, and you will find Him if you seek Him with all your heart and with all your soul. "

Jeremiah said the same thing.

Jeremiah 29:12,13 Then you will call upon Me and go and pray to Me, and I will listen to you. And you will seek Me and find Me, when you search for Me with all your heart.

David agreed.

Psalms 119:2 Blessed are those who keep His testimonies, Who seek Him with the whole heart!

PRAYER AND FASTING

Should We Fast?

Is fasting an Old Testament practice that was under the Old Covenant, and now that we are in the age of grace, not needed?

Jesus said the disciples will fast. He did not say if.

Luke 5: 35 "But the days will come when the bridegroom will be taken away from them; then they will fast in those days."

When the demons wouldn't leave the epileptic boy, Jesus explained to the disciples that the reason was two-fold.

Matthew 17:20a, 21 So Jesus said to them, "Because of your unbelief; ... However, this kind does not go out except by prayer and fasting."

Wrong Motives for Fasting

We aren't to fast in an attempt to force God to hear us. Isaiah describes this erroneous type of fast.

Isaiah 58:3,4 'Why have we fasted,' they say, 'and You have not seen? Why have we afflicted our souls, and You take no notice?'

"In fact, in the day of your fast you find pleasure, and exploit all your laborers. Indeed you fast for strife and debate, and to strike with the fist of wickedness. You will not fast as you do this day, to make your voice heard on high."

We aren't to fast when other areas of our lives aren't pleasing to God.

God's Chosen Fast

God describes the fast He is pleased with.

Isaiah 58:6,7 "Is this not the fast that I have chosen: to loose the bonds of wickedness, to undo the heavy burdens, to let the oppressed go free, and that you break every yoke? Is it not to share your bread with the hungry, and that you bring to your house the poor who are cast out; when you see the naked, that you cover him, and not hide yourself from your own flesh?"

Four Types of Fasting

There are four types of fasting mentioned in the Bible.

➢ *Partial Fast*

Daniel's fast was that he ate no pleasant food, no meat and no wine.

Daniel 10:2,3 In those days I, Daniel, was mourning three full weeks. I ate no pleasant food, no meat or wine came into my mouth, nor did I anoint myself at all, till three whole weeks were fulfilled.

➢ *Normal Fast*

This is a fast where you don't take in food, but do take water or juice. This is normal for a longer fast.

➾ Jesus

Jesus was led by the Holy Spirit into the wilderness and there He fasted forty days. During this fast, we are told He ate nothing.

Luke 4:1,2 Then Jesus, being filled with the Holy Spirit, returned from the Jordan and was led by the Spirit into the wilderness, being tempted for forty days by the devil. And in those days He ate nothing, and afterward, when they had ended, He was hungry.

➢ *Supernatural Fast*

We are told about two supernatural fasts, but these are not a normal pattern for us today.

➪ Elijah

Elijah's fast was different in that he was given food supernaturally and then went on the strength of that food and drink for forty days.

1 Kings 19:5-8 Then as he lay and slept under a broom tree, suddenly an angel touched him, and said to him, "Arise and eat." Then he looked, and there by his head was a cake baked on coals, and a jar of water. So he ate and drank, and lay down again.

And the angel of the LORD came back the second time, and touched him, and said, "Arise and eat, because the journey is too great for you." So he arose, and ate and drank; and he went in the strength of that food forty days and forty nights as far as Horeb, the mountain of God.

➪ Moses

Moses fasted for forty days and nights on the mountain and God gave him the original ten commandments..

Deuteronomy 9:9 "When I went up into the mountain to receive the tablets of stone, the tablets of the covenant which the LORD made with you, then I stayed on the mountain forty days and forty nights. I neither ate bread nor drank water. "

The people worshiped the golden calf – the ten commandments were broken – and Moses returned for another forty days of fasting and praying.

Deuteronomy 9:18 "And I fell down before the LORD, as at the first, forty days and forty nights; I neither ate bread nor drank water, because of all your sin which you committed in doing wickedly in the sight of the LORD, to provoke Him to anger."

Moses' eighty day fast was in the glory of God's presence and is not a pattern for an extended absolute fast today.

➢ Absolute Fast

An absolute fast is usually short in duration and you don't eat any food or take any drink.

➪ The People of Nineveh

When Jonah came to Nineveh, his message was that in forty days the city would be destroyed. The people began an absolute fast. God saw their repentance and didn't destroy the city.

Jonah 3:7b-10 "Let neither man nor beast, herd nor flock, taste anything; do not let them eat, or drink water. But let man and beast be covered with sackcloth, and cry mightily to God; yes, let every one turn from his evil way and from the violence that is in his hands. Who can tell if God will turn and relent, and turn away from His fierce anger, so that we may not perish?"

Then God saw their works, that they turned from their evil way; and God relented from the disaster that He had said He would bring upon them, and He did not do it.

➪ Queen Esther and all the Jews in Shushan

When Queen Esther heard of the threat to her people, she said they were all to fast for three days and that she and her servants would do the same. After the time of fasting, she would go to the king.

Esther 4:16 "Go, gather all the Jews who are present in Shushan, and fast for me; neither eat nor drink for three days, night or day. My maids and I will fast likewise. And so I will go to the king, which is against the law; and if I perish, I perish!"

⇨ Paul

After Paul's encounter with Jesus on the road to Damascus, he fasted in an absolute fast.

Acts 9:9 And he was three days without sight, and neither ate nor drank.

Benefits of Fasting

➢ Demons Leave

Matthew 17:21 "However, this kind does not go out except by prayer and fasting."

➢ National Disaster Adverted

Jonah 3:10 Then God saw their works, that they turned from their evil way; and God relented from the disaster that He had said He would bring upon them, and He did not do it.

➢ Visions Come

Daniel 10:5,6 I lifted my eyes and looked, and behold, a certain man clothed in linen, whose waist was girded with gold of Uphaz! His body was like beryl, his face like the appearance of lightning, his eyes like torches of fire, his arms and feet like burnished bronze in color, and the sound of his words like the voice of a multitude.

➢ Physical Health Restored

Isaiah 58:6-8 "Is this not the fast that I have chosen: to loose the bonds of wickedness, to undo the heavy burdens, to let the oppressed go free, and that you break every yoke?

Then your light shall break forth like the morning, your healing shall spring forth speedily, and your righteousness shall go before you; the glory of the LORD shall be your rear guard."

➢ Pride Brought into Subjection

Psalms 35:13 But as for me, when they were sick, My clothing was sackcloth; I humbled myself with fasting; And my prayer would return to my own heart.

➢ Spiritual Awakening

2 Chronicles 7:14 "if My people who are called by My name will humble themselves, and pray and seek My face, and turn from their wicked ways, then I will hear from heaven, and will forgive their sin and heal their land. "

Should We Fast?

Let's return to our original question – should we fast? With all the benefits we find in Scripture, why wouldn't we want to fast?

Jesus told us to fast in secret.

Matthew 6:16-18 *"Moreover, when you fast, do not be like the hypocrites, with a sad countenance. For they disfigure their faces that they may appear to men to be fasting. Assuredly, I say to you, they have their reward. But you, when you fast, anoint your head and wash your face, so that you do not appear to men to be fasting, but to your Father who is in the secret place; and your Father who sees in secret will reward you openly. "*

Practical Steps to Fasting

Some practical things to know are:

➥ Drink as much water as you can – it is essential.

➥ For a partial fast, eat light food such as fresh fruit. Do not eat processed food. Drink water, milk, or juices. You may want to mix juice (especially citrus) half and half with water.

➥ How long you fast is between you and God. Since fasting is a commitment, a vow, do not make it lightly. It's best to start fasting a meal, or a day from sundown to sundown, and work up to longer periods of time.

➥ A long fast must be broken gradually beginning with juices, and semi-solid food.

✦ Summary – Entering a Successful Prayer Life

To pray successfully, we must develop a life-style of knowing God personally. We must abide in Him. This is much the same as having a good friend over the years. In time, we know in advance how they will think, feel and react to a situation. The more we abide in God, the more we'll know how to ask according to His will.

God desires people to care about the needs around them – to yearn for others to know Him. He desires that His people pray without ceasing, earnestly, intensely, and constantly. He desires those who will seek, labor, and strive for His will to be done.

God has provided the wonderful tool of fasting, with its many benefits, as a method of bringing our bodies and souls into subjection to our spirits and to His Lordship.

QUESTIONS FOR REVIEW

1. What are the four steps to successful praying? Explain each of them briefly.

2. List the benefits of fasting.

3. If you have not fasted before, how will you start? What are your (realistic) goals?

The Voice of Faith

INTRODUCTION

We must pray in faith for our prayers to be answered. In order to do this, we must understand and be people of faith.

We find the word "believe" over one hundred and thirty times in the New Testament. The word "faith" is used over two hundred and twenty times.

Over and over in His earthly ministry, Jesus responded to faith. He said,
"Your faith has made you well."
"According to your faith ..."
"O woman, great is your faith."
"If you have faith and don't doubt ..."
"Have faith in God."

He also said,
"O you of little faith ..."
"Why did you doubt?"
"Because of your unbelief ..."
"How is it you have no faith?"
"Where is your faith?"

To the disciples, He said, "I have prayed for you, that your faith shouldn't fail."

Everything we receive from God, we receive by faith – our salvation, baptism in the Holy Spirit, righteousness, healings, blessings, supernatural wisdom and knowledge.

Faith Speaks

Faith speaks – but what does it say?

The apostle Paul wrote,
Romans 10:6a,8 But the righteousness of faith speaks in this way ... But what does it say? "The word is near you, even in your mouth and in your heart" (that is, the word of faith which we preach).

Faith speaks the Word of God. For our prayers to be answered, we must believe, and to believe we must know God's Word and hear His voice.

This brings us to the question, "What is true faith?"

Before we begin to find that answer, it's important to understand how we are created.

WHO WE ARE

Body, Soul and Spirit

We are made up of three parts:
Body – our bones, flesh and blood
Soul – our intellect, our will, our emotions
Spirit – our life, our being

James said that the body without the spirit is dead.

James 2:26 For as the body without the spirit is dead, so faith without works is dead also.

The writer of the book of Hebrews refers to the soul and the spirit, and said it is by the Word of God that we can tell the soul from the spirit.

Hebrews 4:12 For the word of God is living and powerful, and sharper than any two-edged sword, piercing even to the division of soul and spirit, and of joints and marrow, and is a discerner of the thoughts and intents of the heart.

Paul prayed in Thessalonians that God would sanctify us completely – spirit, soul and body.

1 Thessalonians 5:23 Now may the God of peace Himself sanctify you completely; and may your whole spirit, soul, and body be preserved blameless at the coming of our Lord Jesus Christ.

Born of the Spirit

Our relationship with God is in the spirit. We are born again in the spirit. Many of us try to serve God, to worship Him, to pray to Him from our souls. This cannot be done. We must be born of the Spirit and come to God in the spirit.

John 3:4-6 Nicodemus said to Him, "How can a man be born when he is old? Can he enter a second time into his mother's womb and be born?"

Jesus answered, "Most assuredly, I say to you, unless one is born of water and the Spirit, he cannot enter the kingdom of God. That which is born of the flesh is flesh, and that which is born of the Spirit is spirit."

John reveals to us that God is a Spirit, and that we can only come to Him in the spirit.

John 4:23,24 "But the hour is coming, and now is, when the true worshipers will worship the Father in spirit and truth; for the Father is seeking such to worship Him. God is Spirit, and those who worship Him must worship in spirit and truth."

➤ *A New Creature*

We are to be new creations in the spirit.

2 Corinthians 5:17 Therefore, if anyone is in Christ, he is a new creation; old things have passed away; behold, all things have become new.

One Spirit with God

Through the new birth, we are to be one spirit with God. What we do with God, or for God, must be done in the spirit. Our prayers, to be effective, cannot be prayed in the natural with our minds only, they must also be prayed in the spirit.

1 Corinthians 6:17 But he who is joined to the Lord is one spirit with Him.

We are to serve God with our spirit as the apostle Paul did.

Romans 1:9a For God is my witness, whom I serve with my spirit in the gospel of His Son ...

The writer of the book of Hebrews reveals that we can only please God when we come to Him in faith.

Hebrews 11:6 But without faith it is impossible to please Him, for he who comes to God must believe that He is, and that He is a rewarder of those who diligently seek Him.

NATURAL AND SUPERNATURAL FAITH

Natural Faith

The dictionary says that faith is a confident belief in the truth, value, or trustworthiness of a person, an idea, or a thing. Faith is a natural ability in the area of our souls. For example, when we sit on a chair, we have faith it will hold us up. Most of us operate in natural faith continuously, but this isn't the God-kind of faith revealed in the Bible.

Supernatural Faith

Supernatural faith doesn't rest on logical proof or material evidence, instead it's based on a secure belief in God and in His Word. Supernatural faith is from our spirits – not our minds. Supernatural faith is believing and acting on God's Word without questioning, or trying to reason it out.

Wavering Mind

James described the person who asks in faith, but then begins to doubt. This is a person who goes from believing to not believing, in an endless cycle. He or she is tossed back and forth like a wave in the sea driven by the wind.

James 1:5,6 If any of you lacks wisdom, let him ask of God, who gives to all liberally and without reproach, and it will be given to him. But let him ask in faith, with no doubting, for he who doubts is like a wave of the sea driven and tossed by the wind.

Doubt is the opposite of faith. It's an act of the natural mind. Doubt means to be undecided or skeptical; to tend to disbelieve, or distrust; to regard as unlikely; to be undecided or skeptical; to have a lack of certainty that often leads to irresolution; a lack of trust.

We cannot operate in faith and doubt at the same time. We cannot operate in faith and worry at the same time. They are completely opposite.

Causes of Doubt

There are three main reasons a person battles with doubt which can be recognized and dealt with.

➤ *Lack of Self-Esteem*

One of the major causes for doubt is lack of self-esteem. The most dangerous thing about our lack of self-esteem is that we think we can do nothing about it. "It was the way I was raised, and that's just the way I am," is often heard.

However, in salvation, we became a new creation. We became one spirit with God. A revelation of the new creation leaves no room for a negative self-image.

The apostle Paul tells us even when we were dead in sin, God loved us. Maybe our fathers and mothers didn't love us as they should. Perhaps, they said all sorts of things that were negative and hurtful, but God loved us.

Ephesians 2:4-6 But God, who is rich in mercy, because of His great love with which He loved us, even when we were dead in trespasses, made us alive together with Christ (by grace you have been saved), and raised us up together, and made us sit together in the heavenly places in Christ Jesus.

The prophet Zephaniah gives us a wonderful picture of God rejoicing over us with singing.

Zephaniah 3:17 The LORD your God in your midst, the Mighty One, will save; He will rejoice over you with gladness, He will quiet you in His love, He will rejoice over you with singing.

➪ **We deal with a lack of self-esteem by studying, declaring, and believing God's Word about who we are in Christ.**

➤ *Sin*

The next cause of doubt is sin. Often, it's sin we have managed to hide from our conscious minds. We have convinced ourselves mentally that it's really all right with God, but our spirits are one with God. Our spirits know it's sin. By convincing our minds of error, we have become double-minded.

James 1:6-8 But let him ask in faith, with no doubting, for he who doubts is like a wave of the sea driven and tossed by the wind.

For let not that man suppose that he will receive anything from the Lord; he is a double-minded man, unstable in all his ways.

In 1 Kings we read,
1 Kings 2:4b 'If your sons take heed to their way, to walk before Me in truth with all their heart and with all their soul,' He said, 'you shall not lack a man on the throne of Israel.'

They were to take heed to walk before the Lord in truth with all their heart (spirit) and with all their soul (mind).

➪ **To stop doubt entering through this area, we must recognize sin and confess it. Then it is forgiven and removed.**

1 John 1:9 If we confess our sins, he is faithful and just to forgive us our sins, and to cleanse us from all unrighteousness.

> *Untruthfulness*

The third cause for doubt is a problem which is extremely prevalent today – untruthfulness. Many feel it's really all right to tell "little lies," or "social lies," just to make things go smoother, or to save someone's feelings.

A person who lies, thinks everyone is lying to them. Because they are untruthful, they cannot trust anyone to be truthful. This mistrust extends even to God. Because their word cannot be trusted, they are unable to trust God's Word. They may think and say they do, but in actuality they cannot because of their own character.

King Solomon made how God feels about lying very clear.

Proverbs 6:16-17a These six things the LORD hates, yes, seven are an abomination to Him: A proud look, a lying tongue ...

➥ **To stop doubt from entering through this area, we must make a commitment to become honest, trustworthy children of God.**

We do this by confessing our past lies to God. But also, to break the habit of lying, we need to confess any new lie to the person we lie to. It's surprising how quickly the embarrassment of doing this will teach us to think before we speak.

James 5:16 Confess your faults one to another, and pray one for another, that ye may be healed. The effectual fervent prayer of a righteous man availeth much.

True Faith Based on Truth

Over and over we find the words "in truth" in the Scripture. Joshua wrote,

Joshua 24:14a "Now therefore, fear the LORD, serve Him in sincerity and in truth ..."

The prophet Samuel wrote,
1 Samuel 12:24 "Only fear the LORD, and serve Him in truth with all your heart; for consider what great things He has done for you."

King Solomon wrote,
1 Kings 3:6a And Solomon said: "You have shown great mercy to your servant David my father, because he walked before You in truth, in righteousness, and in uprightness of heart with You."

King Hezekiah prayed,
2 Kings 20:3a "Remember now, O LORD, I pray, how I have walked before You in truth and with a loyal heart, and have done what was good in Your sight."

The apostle John wrote,
1 John 3:18 My little children, let us not love in word or in tongue, but in deed and in truth.

☞ **The works of God can only be done in truth.**

We have been in situations where people seemed to believe "the end justifies the means." They would lie to get money for their needs – even for their ministries – feeling the money was going to "a good cause."

King David wrote,

Psalms 33:4 For the word of the LORD is right, And all His work is done in truth.

Psalms 111:7,8 The works of His hands are verity and justice; All His precepts are sure. They stand fast forever and ever, And are done in truth and uprightness.

THE GOD-KIND OF FAITH

The writer of the book of Hebrews gave us a marvelous chapter on faith in Hebrews 11. It's a roll call of the faithful saints of the Old Testament. No study on faith would be complete without taking time to read this chapter.

Definition

In the book Hebrews, we learn what faith is.

Hebrews 11:1,3 Now faith is the substance of things hoped for, the evidence of things not seen.

By faith we understand that the worlds were framed by the word of God, so that the things which are seen were not made of things which are visible.

Jesus instructed the disciples to have faith in God. He then went on to describe this faith as speaking to the mountain, of not doubting, but of believing.

Mark 11:22-24 So Jesus answered and said to them, "Have faith in God. For assuredly, I say to you, whoever says to this mountain, 'Be removed and be cast into the sea,' and does not doubt in his heart, but believes that those things he says will come to pass, he will have whatever he says. Therefore I say to you, whatever things you ask when you pray, believe that you receive them, and you will have them.

God-Given Faith

True faith is given to us by God, leaving no room for pride.

Ephesians 2:8 For by grace you have been saved through faith, and that not of yourselves; it is the gift of God.

Romans 12:3 For I say, through the grace given to me, to everyone who is among you, not to think of himself more highly than he ought to think, but to think soberly, as God has dealt to each one a measure of faith.

Since God has given each one a measure of faith, can faith grow, or does God give us all we need at one time?

➤ Mustard Seed Faith

Jesus likened faith to a mustard seed – the smallest seed in all the earth. Later, He taught about the mustard seed's ability to grow.

Matthew 17:20b ... for assuredly, I say to you, if you have faith as a mustard seed, you will say to this mountain, 'Move from here to there,' and it will move; and nothing will be impossible for you.

He talked about a mustard seed again.

Mark 4:31,32 "It is like a mustard seed which, when it is sown on the ground, is smaller than all the seeds on earth; but when it is sown, it grows up and becomes greater than all herbs, and shoots out large branches, so that the birds of the air may nest under its shade."

Paul wrote that our faith increases.

2 Corinthians 10:15b ... but having hope, that as your faith is increased, we shall be greatly enlarged by you in our sphere ...

The apostles realized they needed more faith and they prayed,

Luke 17:5b Increase our faith.

The apostle Jude said that we could build up our faith.

Jude 1:20 But you, beloved, building yourselves up on your most holy faith, praying in the Holy Spirit ...

Faith, in our lives, will be as strong as we allow it to be. It will grow over a period of time like the mustard seed.

➢ *Faith Not Hope*

Hope isn't faith. Hope is believing God will act sometime in the future, faith is now. If hope doesn't turn to faith, it will keep us from receiving. "God is going to ... sometime in the future," will keep us from receiving today.

It has been said, "Hope sets the stage, and faith brings the results."

➢ *Faith Not Knowledge*

Knowledge is good. Through knowledge we can make a mental assent – we can agree with our minds that the Word is true. But knowledge without faith will never change our lives. Through faith, knowledge becomes experience.

The apostle Paul wrote,
1 Corinthians 2:9,14 But as it is written: "Eye has not seen, nor ear heard, nor have entered into the heart (mind) of man the things which God has prepared for those who love Him."

But the natural man doesn't receive the things of the Spirit of God, for they are foolishness to him; nor can he know them, because they are spiritually discerned.

Faith Through the Word

Paul said that faith comes by hearing the Word of God. True faith is based on the Word of God. True Faith is knowing the Word of God is more true than anything we hear or see that is contrary to that Word.

Romans 10:17 So then faith comes by hearing, and hearing by the word of God.

Faith comes through our heart attitude of hearing, seeing and understanding in the areas of the spirit. Jesus spoke of those that don't see, don't hear, and don't understand.

Matthew 13:13 *"Therefore I speak to them in parables, because seeing they do not see, and hearing they do not hear, nor do they understand."*

Faith That Overcomes

Faith is extremely important because it will overcome the world.

1 John 5:4 *For whatever is born of God overcomes the world. And this is the victory that has overcome the world – our faith.*

Author of Our Faith

Jesus is the beginning and the end of our faith.

Hebrews 12:2 *looking unto Jesus, the author and finisher of our faith, who for the joy that was set before Him endured the cross, despising the shame, and has sat down at the right hand of the throne of God.*

Where Is Your Faith?

A storm came and the boat was about to sink.

Luke 8:24b,25a *Then He arose and rebuked the wind and the raging of the water. And they ceased, and there was a calm. But He said to them, "Where is your faith?"*

Jesus had told them they were going to the other side. He was in the boat with them and yet when the storm came, they saw only in the natural. "Master, Master, we perish!"

Jesus must still be asking, "Where is our faith?"

Is it in the natural, or in the supernatural? Our faith should be based on the Word of God, in our spirit, and in our mouth.

Romans 10:8 *But what does it say? "The word is near you, even in your mouth and in your heart" (that is, the word of faith which we preach).*

The Gift of Faith

The gift of faith is a supernatural gift of the Holy Spirit which usually comes through receiving a word of wisdom for a particular person, time or situation. It is one of the power gifts of the Holy Spirit and allows us to move into the working of miracles and gifts of healings.

Enemies of Faith

➤ *We Must Fight*

The apostle Paul encouraged Timothy to fight the good fight of faith. The word "fight" certainly infers there are enemies of our faith.

1 Timothy 6:12 *Fight the good fight of faith, lay hold on eternal life, to which you were also called and have confessed the good confession in the presence of many witnesses.*

➤ *Natural Senses*

Our natural senses are the strongest enemies of faith. Trusting what we see, hear, and touch more than we trust the Word of God, will defeat us.

The Word of God is true. God will do what His Word says. The words of those who don't believe, the symptoms we still see or feel in our bodies, the unpaid bills, don't change the Word of God. Paul wrote about this.

Romans 3:3,4a For what if some did not believe? Will their unbelief make the faithfulness of God without effect?

Certainly not! Indeed, let God be true but every man a liar.

➤ *Unbelief*

Unbelief is a strong enemy but it will not change God's Word. It will just stop the Word from being true in our own lives.

The writer of the book of Hebrews said that faith is the evidence of things not seen and he used Noah as his example.

Hebrews 11:1,7 Now faith is the substance of things hoped for, the evidence of things not seen.

By faith Noah, being divinely warned of things not yet seen, moved with godly fear, prepared an ark for the saving of his household, by which he condemned the world and became heir of the righteousness which is according to faith.

The apostle Paul also referred to things that aren't seen.

2 Corinthians 4:18 while we do not look at the things which are seen, but at the things which are not seen. For the things which are seen are temporary, but the things which are not seen are eternal.

➤ *Doubt*

Thomas had a hard time moving from the realm of the natural to the supernatural – from unbelief to belief. He said, "Unless I see, unless I touch, I will not believe."

John 20:24-29 But Thomas, called Didymus, one of the twelve, was not with them when Jesus came. The other disciples therefore said to him, "We have seen the Lord."

But he said to them, "Unless I see in His hands the print of the nails, and put my finger into the print of the nails, and put my hand into His side, I will not believe."

And after eight days His disciples were again inside, and Thomas with them. Jesus came, the doors being shut, and stood in the midst, and said, "Peace to you!" Then He said to Thomas, "Reach your finger here, and look at My hands; and reach your hand here, and put it into My side. Do not be unbelieving, but believing."

And Thomas answered and said to Him, "My Lord and my God!"

Jesus said to him, "Thomas, because you have seen Me, you have believed. Blessed are those who have not seen and yet have believed."

Thomas' demand to see and touch before he would believe, has become an example to us of what not to do. He did go on from that time to become an apostle of the gospel and to die a martyr's death, but he has still been referred to throughout history as Doubting Thomas.

PRAYER OF FAITH, AGREEMENT AND PRAYING THE WORD

To be effective, prayer must be based on faith. That is the reason we have spent time studying what faith is and how it operates.

Prayer of Faith

James spoke of the prayer of faith that would save the sick. There is only one mention of this specific type of prayer in the Scriptures. Notice that the person needing prayer, asks for it. Notice also that sin may be involved and needs to be forgiven. The elders mentioned here are the leaders of the local church who will come and pray in faith.

James 5:14,15 Is anyone among you sick? Let him call for the elders of the church, and let them pray over him, anointing him with oil in the name of the Lord. And the prayer of faith will save the sick, and the Lord will raise him up. And if he has committed sins, he will be forgiven.

What is the prayer of faith? It's a prayer that is based solidly on the promises of God and prayed in faith. It's also based on two or more being in agreement.

When the prayer of faith has been prayed, there is a witness of the Holy Spirit that it's done. The truth of God's Word is more real to us than the symptoms or circumstances. This faith is from our spirits not our minds. From the moment this faith comes, we stand in faith on God's Word being accomplished.

Power of Agreement

Power and authority are multiplied when two or more believers unite their faith in a prayer of agreement.

Deuteronomy 32:30 How could one chase a thousand, and two put ten thousand to flight, unless their Rock had sold them, and the LORD had surrendered them?

Prayers of Agreement

The prayer of agreement is based on Jesus' teaching about two agreeing and asking God together.

Matthew 18:19,20 "Again I say to you that if two of you agree on earth concerning anything that they ask, it will be done for them by My Father in heaven. For where two or three are gathered together in My name, I am there in the midst of them."

To be in agreement, we must know what the situation is, what the answer is from the Word of God, and then ask in one accord. For example, we cannot pray the prayer of agreement with someone who has "an unspoken request."

➢ *Focus Our Prayers*

Perhaps one of the greatest benefits of coming into a prayer of agreement is that it causes us to focus our prayers on certain objectives. Remember the blind beggars who cried out to Jesus, "Have mercy on us, O Lord, Son of David!"

What did Jesus reply? "What do you want Me to do for you?"

Did they want money? Did they want jobs? Did they want to be healed? Where was there faith?

We need to be specific in our requests, because this helps us focus our faith for maximum results.

➢ *Remove Doubt and Unbelief*

When Jesus came to Jarius' house, He removed the doubters before He raised the child from the dead.

Mark 5:39-42   When He came in, He said to them, "Why make this commotion and weep? The child is not dead, but sleeping."

And they laughed Him to scorn.

But when He had put them all out, He took the father and the mother of the child, and those who were with Him, and entered where the child was lying. Then He took the child by the hand, and said to her, "Talitha, cumi," which is translated, "Little girl, I say to you, arise." Immediately the girl arose and walked, for she was twelve years of age. And they were overcome with great amazement.

➢ *Pray Together*

Earlier we mentioned that some prayers weren't answered because they weren't prayed. This happens if we're not careful in the prayer of agreement. We talk over a situation, quote the Word of God that applies to it, and agree how we will pray. At the moment we come into agreement – with each other and the will of God – we must ask together in a unity of faith believing it will be done.

This doesn't mean one prays and the others agree. They are both, or all, to pray agreeing in what they pray. There is no example in the Bible of one being asked to lead in prayer, while others listen or agree.

Praying God's Word

➢ *The Word Is Alive*

The writer of the book of Hebrews tells us that God's Word is alive and powerful.

Hebrews 4:12 (Amp) For the word that God speaks is alive and full of power – making it active, operative, energizing and effective; it is sharper than any two-edged sword, penetrating to the dividing line of the breath of life (soul) and spirit, and of joints and marrow, exposing and sifting and analyzing and judging the very thoughts and purpose of the heart.

The prophet Jeremiah said that God watches over His Word to perform it.

Jeremiah 1:12 (Amp) Then said the LORD to me, "You have seen well, for I am alert and active, watching over My word to perform it."

> *Pray the Solution*

Praying God's Word is one of the most forceful ways we have to stop ourselves from praying the problem. Instead, we pray the solution.

The prophet Isaiah gave us a great insight into what happens when God's Word goes forth.

Isaiah 55:11 So shall My word be that goes forth from My mouth; it shall not return to Me void, but it shall accomplish what I please, and it shall prosper in the thing for which I sent it.

God's Word will not return empty. It will accomplish what it was sent to do.

When we pray the Word in a particular situation, we should take time to find the promises of God that apply. Promise books are great to use in this way. It's good to write God's promises down so that we can go through them as we pray. (God never said we should close our eyes and pray. The only reason to do so is to avoid distractions so we can focus on God)

> *For Healing*

If we need healing, there is no need to tell God how awful we feel, about what the doctors say, or about the things we are supposed to be doing that aren't getting done. Our prayers should be something like this,

"Lord, I thank You that Your Word says Jesus was wounded for my transgression, He was bruised for my iniquities: that the chastisement of my peace was upon Him; that by His stripes I am healed. Thank You Lord, that through Jeremiah You said You would restore health unto me, and heal me of my wounds. Thank You that it's Your desire above all things that I would be in good health. Thank You Lord! I believe and I receive the full manifestation of my healing right now!

  * Isaiah 53:5, Jeremiah 30:17, 3 John 2

> *For Our Loved Ones*

Perhaps we have loved ones who aren't close to the Lord. Again, there is no need to tell God where they are or what they are doing. How do we pray for them? By praying the Word.

"Father, I thank You that Your Word says that You aren't slack concerning Your promise but You are longsuffering to us, unwilling that any should perish, but that all should come to repentance. God you are unwilling that ... should perish. Thank You that You have promised me that if I believe on the Lord Jesus Christ I would be saved and all my house. Father, Your Word says that if we train up a child in the way he should go, when he is old, he will not depart from it. I thank You ..."

  * 2 Peter 3:9, Acts 16:31, Proverbs 22:6

> *For Finances*

You might consider putting your bills together on your desk along with your checkbook. Lay your hands on them and begin to pray.

"Father, You know every bill that is here and every bill that is coming in. You know the dates they are due and the amounts. I thank You, Lord that Your Word says that if we bring all the tithes into the storehouse, You will open the windows of heaven and pour out so many blessings there will not be room enough to receive them. I rejoice in Your promise that You would rebuke the devourer for my sake. How wonderful it is, God, that You said You wished above all things that I would prosper even as my soul prospers. Father Your Word says, You are my Shepherd and I should not want. I thank You Lord ..."

* *Malachi 3:10,11,3 John 2, Psalm 23:1*

✦ Summary – The Voice of Faith

We are body, soul, and spirit. We are born again of the Spirit. Before we were born again, we had faith, but it was in the natural realm. Now we are in the kingdom of God and our faith is supernatural. Our faith is based on what the Word of God says, not on what we see around us. We are no longer going to live with negative self-images. We are going to see ourselves as God sees us. No longer are we going to let sin and untruthfulness bring doubt to our lives.

We are going to exercise our God-given faith. We are going to have faith in God's Word. We are going to have faith that overcomes. We are going to agree with others in prayers of faith and agreement. We are going to pray God's Word and experience the marvelous things that God will do for us!

QUESTIONS FOR REVIEW

1. Since we are made up of body, soul and spirit, how do we know if our faith is from the soul area (the mind, will and emotions), or from the spirit?

2. Give a definition in your own words of the God-kind of faith.

3. What is meant by the prayer of faith and the prayer of agreement?

4. Write a brief example of praying the Word for someone you are concerned about.

Lesson Eight

Praying in Authority

INTRODUCTION

Many prayers aren't answered because we are pleading with God to do something He has told us to do. We are to live and rule on this earth as Adam and Eve were created to do. We have had the concept that prayer is limited to asking, but a very important part of prayer is listening. When we listen, God will tell us what to do – what to say – what to command – what to speak into existence.

Prayer is asking – listening – obeying. These are the same elements as in military life, where we ask the commander what to do, hear the orders he gives, and then obey.

In Lesson Two we studied the creation of mankind and the authority God delegated to them. In this lesson we will learn how to put this authority into practice in our prayer life.

It's God's desire that believers begin to move in life-changing authority on this earth. He is looking for men and women who will move in authority totally under His control.

Practical Steps

In this lesson, we will discover practical steps to moving in authority. The people God can use to pray authoritative prayers are:

⇨ **Vessels empty of their own desires**

⇨ **Those who have the humble heart of a servant**

Authoritative prayers will be:

⇨ **Based on hearing from God through the revelation gifts of the Holy Spirit**

⇨ **Spoken forcefully through the gift of faith given by the Holy Spirit**

Forceful, authoritative, kingly prayers never come from an attitude of "Wouldn't it be nice if." For example, "Wouldn't it be nice if it didn't rain on Sunday since we are having a church picnic." Some would even say, "In the name of Jesus, I command the weather to be nice on Sunday." Stop! Authoritative prayers can never come from our own desires or wills. Elijah stopped the rain and it wouldn't start again until he said to, but he was totally under the direction of God.

1 Kings 17:1 And Elijah the Tishbite, of the inhabitants of Gilead, said to Ahab, "As the LORD God of Israel lives, before whom I stand, there shall not be dew nor rain these years, except at my word."

The apostle James referred to this time,
James 5:17,18 Elijah was a man with a nature like ours, and he prayed earnestly that it would not rain; and it did not rain on the land for three years

and six months. And he prayed again, and the heaven gave rain, and the earth produced its fruit.

Notice there was both prayer and declaration. He prayed and heard from God and then he declared with authority, "There shall not be rain these years, except at my word."

JESUS OUR EXAMPLE

In everything we do, Jesus, the Last Adam, must always be our example. On earth, Jesus did everything the first Adam was created to do. We can truly say, "If Jesus did it, we can do it too!" We can do it through His name, and through the power of the Holy Spirit.

Empowered by the Holy Spirit

Jesus did no miracles until He was baptized and the Holy Spirit came upon Him. Luke tells us,

Luke 4:14-19 Then Jesus returned in the power of the Spirit to Galilee, ... And as His custom was, He went into the synagogue on the Sabbath day, and stood up to read ...

And when He had opened the book, He found the place where it was written: "The Spirit of the Lord is upon Me, because He has anointed Me to preach the gospel to the poor. He has sent Me to heal the brokenhearted, to preach deliverance to the captives and recovery of sight to the blind, to set at liberty those who are oppressed, to preach the acceptable year of the Lord."

We too must be empowered by the Holy Spirit.

Gave Authority to Believers

During His ministry on earth, Jesus had authority over demons, sickness and disease, the human body, creation, the elements, and even death. He has given this authority to us.

According to John, He said,
John 14:12 "Most assuredly, I say to you, he who believes in Me, the works that I do he will do also; and greater works than these he will do, because I go to My Father."

According to Matthew, He said,
Matthew 10:8 "Heal the sick, cleanse the lepers, raise the dead, cast out demons. Freely you have received, freely give."

According to Luke, He said,
Luke 10:19 "Behold, I give you the authority to trample on serpents and scorpions, and over all the power of the enemy, and nothing shall by any means hurt you."

Jesus took back the authority Satan had taken from Adam and Eve and He gave it to His followers – to believers – to us!

➢ *Over Demons*

Jesus had authority over the demons.

Matthew 8:31,32 So the demons begged Him, saying, "If You cast us out, permit us to go away into the herd of swine."

And He said to them, "Go." So when they had come out, they went into the herd of swine. And suddenly the whole herd of swine ran violently down the steep place into the sea, and perished in the water.

Jesus didn't plead with God to take care of the demons. He said, "Go."

➤ *Over Sickness and Disease*

The leper came to Jesus and he was cleansed.

Mark 1:40,41 Then a leper came to Him, imploring Him, kneeling down to Him and saying to Him, "If You are willing, You can make me clean."

And Jesus, moved with compassion, put out His hand and touched him, and said to him, "I am willing; be cleansed."

Jesus didn't plead with God to heal him. He said "Be cleansed."

➤ *Over the Human Body*

A man with a withered hand approached Jesus.

Mark 3:3,5b Then He said to the man who had the withered hand, "Step forward." ... "Stretch out your hand." And he stretched it out, and his hand was restored as whole as the other.

Again we don't see Jesus asking God to perform a sovereign act and supernaturally heal this man. He said "Stretch out your hand."

➤ *Over Creation*

Jesus had authority over the fig tree, a part of creation.

Matthew 21:19 And seeing a fig tree by the road, He came to it and found nothing on it but leaves, and said to it, "Let no fruit grow on you ever again." And immediately the fig tree withered away.

➤ *Over the Elements*

Jesus spoke to the wind and the sea and they obeyed Him.

Mark 4:37-39 And a great windstorm arose, and the waves beat into the boat, so that it was already filling. But He was in the stern, asleep on a pillow. And they awoke Him and said to Him, "Teacher, do You not care that we are perishing?"

Then He arose and rebuked the wind, and said to the sea, "Peace, be still!" And the wind ceased and there was a great calm.

➤ *Over Death*

Jesus stood in front of the grave of Lazarus and took authority over death.

John 11:43b,44 He cried with a loud voice, "Lazarus, come forth!" And he who had died came out bound hand and foot with graveclothes, and his face was wrapped with a cloth. Jesus said to them, "Loose him, and let him go."

THE VOICE OF AUTHORITY

In the last lesson we studied the voice of faith. Now we should consider the voice of authority. Did you notice how brief the words of Jesus were in the above examples?

Jesus said, "Go." "Be cleansed." "Stretch out your hand." "Let no fruit grow on you ever again." "Peace, be still!" "Lazarus, come forth!"

The Centurion

When the centurion came to Jesus, He said, "Only speak a word, and my servant will be healed."

Matthew 8:8-10 The centurion answered and said, "Lord, I am not worthy that You should come under my roof. But only speak a word, and my servant will be healed. For I also am a man under authority, having soldiers under me. And I say to this one, 'Go,' and he goes; and to another, 'Come,' and he comes; and to my servant, 'Do this,' and he does it."

When Jesus heard it, He marveled, and said to those who followed, "Assuredly, I say to you, I have not found such great faith, not even in Israel!"

The centurion recognized the authority in Jesus because he was also under authority. Notice the brevity of the centurion's examples – "Go," "Come," "Do this."

Be Brief

The voice of authority is brief. There are no explanations. There are no qualifying remarks.

Remember Jesus' words:
Matthew 6:7,8 (Amp) "And when you pray do not (multiply words, repeating the same ones over and over, and) heap up phrases as the Gentiles do, for they think they will be heard for their much speaking. Do not be like them, for your Father knows what you need before you ask Him."

➢ *Let Words Be Few*

In Ecclesiastes we read,
Ecclesiastes 5:2 Do not be rash with your mouth, and let not your heart utter anything hastily before God. For God is in heaven, and you on earth; therefore let your words be few.

➢ *Biblical Examples*

➪ **Daniel uttered a prayer that is classic in its brevity.**

Daniel 9:19 "O Lord, hear! O Lord, forgive! O Lord, listen and act! Do not delay for Your own sake, my God, for Your city and Your people are called by Your name."

➪ **Moses also had prayers that were wonderfully concise.**

Numbers 10:35,36 So it was, whenever the ark set out, that Moses said: "Rise up, O LORD! Let Your enemies be scattered, and let those who hate You flee before You."

And when it rested, he said: "Return, O LORD, to the many thousands of Israel."

⟹ **Another example of a brief prayer is that of Elijah raising a child from the dead.**

1 Kings 17:21,22 And he stretched himself out on the child three times, and cried out to the LORD and said, "O LORD my God, I pray, let this child's soul come back to him."

Then the LORD heard the voice of Elijah; and the soul of the child came back to him, and he revived.

Elijah's Encounter with Priests of Baal

We discussed Elijah's encounter with the priests of Baal in Lesson Five. Elijah was certainly a man who understood authority. After the people of Israel had watched Baal's priests leaping, shouting, crying, and cutting themselves for a whole day, they saw that nothing happened.

After Elijah had prepared the altar and the sacrifice, he came near and said ... He didn't shout – he didn't leap – he didn't plead – he didn't cut himself – he prayed sixty-four short words, one time.

1 Kings 18:36-38 And it came to pass, at the time of the offering of the evening sacrifice, that Elijah the prophet came near and said, "LORD God of Abraham, Isaac, and Israel, let it be known this day that You are God in Israel, and that I am Your servant, and that I have done all these things at Your word. Hear me, O LORD, hear me, that this people may know that You are the LORD God, and that You have turned their hearts back to You again."

Then the fire of the LORD fell and consumed the burnt sacrifice, and the wood and the stones and the dust, and it licked up the water that was in the trench.

WHO CAN GOD USE?

The Humble

Moses was brought up as the son of Pharaoh's daughter. He knew riches and authority. Then he fled into the desert, and God appeared to him in a burning bush. Moses certainly walked in authority. He brought the plagues on Egypt. He parted the Red Sea. He brought water from the rock in the desert. He talked to God on the mountain. He was so close to God that his face was transformed. If ever a person had cause to think highly of himself, Moses did. But we read in Numbers,

Numbers 12:3 (Now the man Moses was very humble, more than all men who were on the face of the earth.)

Because Moses was so humble, God could allow him to move in powerful supernatural authority.

The Servant

Jesus said,
Matthew 20:26,27 "Yet it shall not be so among you; but whoever desires to become great among you, let him be your servant. And whoever desires to be first among you, let him be your slave."

The Imitator of Christ

They had partaken of the last Passover Feast when Jesus – the Son of God – the One facing horrible betrayal and crucifixion on the cross – washed the disciple's feet. Jesus washed the feet of Judas even though He knew Judas was about to betray Him.

Jesus had to be preparing Himself mentally and emotionally for His trial and death. Why did He take time that evening to wash their feet?

He answered this question for us. He did it as an example for them, and surely, also for us. The disciples were to be servants to one another. We too are to be servants to one another.

John 13:3-5,12-15 Jesus, knowing that the Father had given all things into His hands, and that He had come from God and was going to God, rose from supper and laid aside His garments, took a towel and girded Himself. After that, He poured water into a basin and began to wash the disciples' feet, and to wipe them with the towel with which He was girded.

So when He had washed their feet, taken His garments, and sat down again, He said to them, "Do you know what I have done to you? You call me Teacher and Lord, and you say well, for so I am.

If I then, your Lord and Teacher, have washed your feet, you also ought to wash one another's feet. For I have given you an example, that you should do as I have done to you."

The Available

We tend to put an aura or illusion around persons and events when we read about them in the Bible. We regard them with reverence and awe. We must stop doing this because it prevents us from picturing ourselves doing the things they did. God placed the events in their lives in the Bible to be examples for us. We read of their great victories and failures, so that we can see them as people, like ourselves, operating in the power of God.

Elijah was one of the most powerful men of God, and yet the apostle James wrote some very encouraging words when he said he was a man with a nature like ours.

James 5:17a Elijah was a man with a nature like ours, and he prayed earnestly that it would not rain ...

The Prepared Vessel

We can prepare ourselves and be vessels of honor, useful for the Master, prepared for every good work.

2 Timothy 2:20,21 But in a great house there are not only vessels of gold and silver, but also of wood and clay, some for honor and some for dishonor. Therefore if anyone cleanses himself from the latter, he will be a vessel for honor, sanctified and useful for the Master, prepared for every good work.

POWER TO PRAY IN THE NAME OF JESUS

The Name above All Names

The name of Jesus is above all names.

Philippians 2:8-11 And being found in appearance as a man, He humbled Himself and became obedient to the point of death, even the death of the cross. Therefore God also has highly exalted Him and given Him the name which is above every name, that at the name of Jesus every knee should bow, of those in heaven, and of those on earth, and of those under the earth, and that every tongue should confess that Jesus Christ is Lord, to the glory of God the Father.

Authority in His Name

The authority Jesus gave to the disciples was to use His name.

Mark 16:15-18 And He said to them, "Go into all the world and preach the gospel to every creature. He who believes and is baptized will be saved; but he who does not believe will be condemned. And these signs will follow those who believe: In My name they will cast out demons; they will speak with new tongues; they will take up serpents; and if they drink anything deadly, it will by no means hurt them; they will lay hands on the sick, and they will recover."

Ask in His Name

We are to ask in His name.

John 15:16 "You did not choose Me, but I chose you and appointed you that you should go and bear fruit, and that your fruit should remain, that whatever you ask the Father in My name He may give you."

John 14:13,14 "And whatever you ask in My name, that I will do, that the Father may be glorified in the Son. If you ask anything in My name, I will do it."

Miracle Done in His Name

The first miracle the disciples did after Jesus returned to the Father was in His name.

Acts 3:1-8 Now Peter and John went up together to the temple at the hour of prayer, the ninth hour. And a certain man lame from his mother's womb was carried, whom they laid daily at the gate of the temple which is called Beautiful, to ask alms from those who entered the temple; who, seeing Peter and John about to go into the temple, asked for alms.

And fixing his eyes on him, with John, Peter said, "Look at us." So he gave them his attention, expecting to receive something from them.

Then Peter said, "Silver and gold I do not have, but what I do have I give you: In the name of Jesus Christ of Nazareth, rise up and walk." And he took him by the right hand and lifted him up, and immediately his feet and ankle bones received strength. So he, leaping up, stood and walked and entered the temple with them – walking, leaping, and praising God.

Notice the authority with which Peter spoke, "In the name of Jesus, rise up and walk." He didn't ask God to heal the man.

Do Everything in His Name

We are to do everything we do in the name of Jesus.

Colossians 3:17 And whatever you do in word or deed, do all in the name of the Lord Jesus, giving thanks to God the Father through Him.

WARFARE PRAYERS

Jesus said He only did what He saw the Father doing.

John 5:19 Then Jesus answered and said to them, "Most assuredly, I say to you, the Son can do nothing of Himself, but what He sees the Father do; for whatever He does, the Son also does in like manner. "

To operate in the powerful authority God has for us and that the world so desperately needs, we must do only what the Father says to do. We must lay aside our own desires. We must lay aside anything that would hinder us from knowing His will.

We are to operate in the power of the Holy Spirit just as Jesus did. We are to pray in the spirit until we know what His will is.

In faith, we are to be the voice of faith speaking God's will forth into existence.

Three Warnings

There are three warnings we must remember.

➥ **God will absolutely never tell us to speak or do something that is contrary to His written Word.**

The Word is God and God can never contradict Himself.

John 1:1 In the beginning was the Word, and the Word was with God, and the Word was God.

➥ **God will never tell us to speak or do something for our own glory or profit.**

One of the temptations Satan brought to Jesus was just this. Jesus could have proved He was the Son of God with just one act. He could have avoided the cross and taken over the rulership of this world with no sacrifice.

Matthew 4:5,6 Then the devil took Him up into the holy city, set Him on the pinnacle of the temple, and said to Him, "If You are the Son of God, throw Yourself down. For it is written: 'He shall give His angels charge concerning you,' and, 'In their hands they shall bear you up, lest you dash your foot against a stone.'"

➥ **God will never tell us to take authority over another person, violating his or her free volition.**

God will, at times, allow us to take authority over demons that control another person.

The Gates Shall Not Prevail

We are at war with demonic forces. When Jesus mentioned the word "church" for the first time, He said the gates of Hades wouldn't prevail over it. These gates represent the governments of hell. Jesus said the demonic forces wouldn't prevail against His church.

Matthew 16:18 "And I also say to you that you are Peter, and on this rock I will build My church, and the gates of Hades shall not prevail against it."

Binding and Loosing

Jesus has given us the power to bind and loose.

Matthew 16:19 "And I will give you the keys of the kingdom of heaven, and whatever you bind on earth will be bound in heaven, and whatever you loose on earth will be loosed in heaven."

To bind means to limit Satan or a demon ruler over a particular situation where God has led us into spiritual warfare. We are to bind the strong man.

Matthew 12:28,29 "But if I cast out demons by the Spirit of God, surely the kingdom of God has come upon you. Or else how can one enter a strong man's house and plunder his goods, unless he first binds the strong man? And then he will plunder his house."

Jesus gave us an example of binding and loosing.

Luke 13:11,12,16 And behold, there was a woman who had a spirit of infirmity eighteen years, and was bent over and could in no way raise herself up. But when Jesus saw her, He called her to Him and said to her, "Woman, you are loosed from your infirmity."

"So ought not this woman, being a daughter of Abraham, whom Satan has bound – think of it – for eighteen years, be loosed from this bond on the Sabbath?"

As believers, we have been given realms of authority where we live and are sent by God. In these realms, we have authority to either bind or loose. Through strong authoritative prayers, we can release the power and ability of God to work on earth.

Wrestling Against Principalities

We should always remember our warfare isn't against other human beings. We wrestle with the forces of hell.

Ephesians 6:12 For we do not wrestle against flesh and blood, but against principalities, against powers, against the rulers of the darkness of this age, against spiritual hosts of wickedness in the heavenly places.

Pulling Down Strongholds

The weapons of our warfare are the name of Jesus, the blood of Jesus, and the Word of God. These are weapons of the spirit, and they are mighty.

2 Corinthians 10:4,5 For the weapons of our warfare are not carnal but mighty in God for pulling down strongholds, casting down arguments and every high thing that exalts itself against the knowledge of God, bringing every thought into captivity to the obedience of Christ.

Taking the Kingdom by Force

In our prayers, we are to forcefully advance the kingdom of God. We are to say with boldness and authority, "Thy kingdom come!

Thy will be done! On earth as it is in heaven." These are kingly prayers which bring the kingdom of heaven and His will to earth. We are the violent who must take the kingdom by force.

Matthew 11:12 *"And from the days of John the Baptist until now the kingdom of heaven suffers violence, and the violent take it by force."*

Jesus Is Waiting

In the Psalms David prophesied,
Psalms 110:1 *The LORD said to my Lord, "Sit at My right hand, Till I make Your enemies Your footstool."*

Matthew, Mark and Luke all recorded Jesus quoting these words of David.

Luke 20:42,43 *"Now David himself said in the Book of Psalms, 'The Lord said to my Lord, "sit at My right hand, till I make Your enemies Your footstool."'*

After the Holy Spirit had come on the Day of Pentecost, Peter preached his first sermon and 3,000 souls were added to the church. In this sermon, Peter also quoted David (Acts 2:34,35).

The writer of the book of Hebrews quoted this prophecy of David.

Hebrews 10:12 *But this Man, after He had offered one sacrifice for sins forever, sat down at the right hand of God, from that time waiting till His enemies are made His footstool.*

Six times our attention is called to this one truth. Why?

We know Jesus is interceding for us in heaven, but do we also understand that He is waiting for us to do something? He is waiting for His enemies to be made His footstool – to be put under His feet!

◆ Summary – Praying in Authority

**On the cross, Jesus cried with a loud voice, "It is finished!"
Jesus has paid the penalty for the sin of mankind.
Jesus, through the shedding of His blood, has redeemed us from the curse of the law.
Jesus has purchased back our authority.**

**Now, Jesus is waiting for us to make His enemies His footstool!
He has given us His name. He has given us the power of the Holy Spirit.
He has given us authority. Now, it is up to us!
Through prayer, we must forcefully bring the kingdom of God to earth.**

QUESTIONS FOR REVIEW

1. In Matthew 8:8, why did the centurion tell Jesus that He didn't need to come to his house to heal his servant, but that He could speak a word and heal him? How is this an example for us today?

2. What types of prayers are the words, "Go" "Come!" "Arise and be healed."

3. How do you know if God is releasing you to pray an authoritative prayer?

Lesson Nine

The Heart-Cry of God

INTRODUCTION

All through the Bible, the heart-cry of God is revealed as He calls on His people to intercede. It is found in the words of Ezekiel as he wrote about God seeking for a man to intercede and how He found no one.

Ezekiel 22:30 "So I sought for a man among them who would make a wall, and stand in the gap before Me on behalf of the land, that I should not destroy it; but I found no one."

In Chronicles we read the heart-cry of God for His people to intercede. He said that if they would humble themselves, turn from their wickedness and pray, He could heal their land.

2 Chronicles 7:14 "if My people who are called by My name will humble themselves, and pray and seek My face, and turn from their wicked ways, then I will hear from heaven, and will forgive their sin and heal their land."

Jesus told the disciples that the harvest was great but the laborers were few. What were they to do? Pray!

Luke 10:2 Then He said to them, "The harvest truly is great, but the laborers are few; therefore pray the Lord of the harvest to send out laborers into His harvest."

There are more verses in the Bible on intercession than all the other types of prayers. Prayers of authority are often based on the supernatural knowledge that comes to us through intercession.

The first examples of prayer, starting with the book Job, are those of intercession. The Patriarchs interceded for their families. The godly leaders of the country interceded for their country and people. The priests interceded. Jesus interceded. The apostles interceded. We are to continue the line of Christ-like men and women interceding for our families, government leaders, and leaders in the body of Christ.

Definition of Intercession

Intercession means to go before God on behalf of another person even to the point of taking another's place. True intercession comes from deep within our being. It comes from having such a close personal relationship with God that we can feel His concerns, His desires, and then, as He leads, release His power into the lives of others.

Intercession is made for people and it is to be the priestly function of every believer.

Wilson Mamboleo wrote, "Intercessors stand between God and the person or group of people who need intercession. They forget about their own needs and identify themselves with the welfare of the individual or group they are praying for. They feel another's pains as if they were their own. They find it a delight to pray for other people's needs. There is a lot of joy in the hearts of the intercessors when they are praying for others. Their hearts receive inward spiritual strength. God is pleased with them. Intercessors are men and women to whom God can reveal His secrets and plans for a family, church and nation."

*Taken from **Meeting with God – Prayer's Deepest Meaning**. Published by Prayer and Word Publications, Nairobi, Kenya, Africa.*

Practical Steps of Intercession

When you are interceding there are six basic steps it's good to remember.

↪ **Be specific, do not pray aimlessly.**

↪ **Find the promises of God that fit the need and base your prayers on these. This will keep your prayers in line with God's Will.**

↪ **Allow the Holy Spirit to pray through you.**

↪ **Don't base your prayers on a person's goodness. They have none of their own. Righteousness is based on a believer's position in Christ. Always intercede on the basis of God's grace and mercy.**

↪ **Don't try to control people in prayer or make decisions for them. God will never violate their free volition and you are not allowed to do so either.**

↪ **Be persistent – don't give up!**

Satan's Strategy

Satan has a plan of attack on every believer who moves into God-led intercession. He tries to twist what God reveals and make the intercessor feel he or she is to instruct the leaders on the ways of God. He will try to trick the intercessor into usurping a position of leadership or even of control.

An intercessor must be continuously on guard against a judgmental attitude, and a condemning or controlling spirit.

BIBLICAL EXAMPLES OF INTERCESSION

One of the best ways to learn how to intercede is by studying biblical examples.

Jesus Intercedes for Us

Jesus is always our best example.

➢ Our High Priest

Old Testament priests were a picture of the intercessor. They stood between man and God, making sacrifices for the sins of the people. Jesus is our High Priest and our example of praying for others as He continues to live and make intercession.

Hebrews 7:25 Therefore He is also able to save to the uttermost those who come to God through Him, since He ever lives to make intercession for them.

➤ *Our Advocate, or Intercessor*

The dictionary says that an advocate is one who speaks, pleads, or argues in favor of; one that pleads in another's behalf; a supporter or defender. Jesus is all that and more for us.

1 John 2:1 My little children, these things I write to you, that you may not sin. And if anyone sins, we have an Advocate with the Father, Jesus Christ the righteous.

➤ *Expressed the Heart-Cry of God*

Through Jesus we have two examples which show us the heart-cry of God. The first was Jesus crying over the people of Jerusalem.

Luke 13:34 "O Jerusalem, Jerusalem, the one who kills the prophets and stones those who are sent to her! How often I wanted to gather your children together, as a hen gathers her brood under her wings, but you were not willing!"

Notice that Jesus, even in His great love, didn't control them. He said, "But you were not willing."

The second great example happened as Jesus hung on the cross.

Luke 23:33a,34a And when they had come to the place called Calvary, there they crucified Him ... Then Jesus said, "Father, forgive them, for they do not know what they do."

If anyone had a right to be condemning, Jesus did. The people of Jerusalem had killed the prophets and stoned the messengers, but Jesus' only desire was to hold them under the wings of His protection. Even when they had crucified Him, His prayer was, "Father, forgive them."

It is important when we are interceding that we do not become ensnared in Satan's devices. No matter how much God shows us what is wrong, we must not judge or condemn, but instead use that knowledge for intercession.

Job Interceded

Job is considered to be the oldest book in the Bible, and Job was an intercessor.

When calamities fell on Job, his friends came, but they thought evil of him, criticized him and tried to figure out in their own minds why such horrible things could happen. They came out of concern, but they stayed to condemn.

When the time of testing was over, God told them to offer a burnt offering, and then to humble themselves and go to the one they had criticized and ask him to intercede for them.

Job 42:8-10 "Now therefore, take for yourselves seven bulls and seven rams, go to My servant Job, and offer up for yourselves a burnt offering; and My servant Job shall pray for you. For I will accept him, lest I deal with you according to your folly; because you have not spoken of Me what is right, as My servant Job has."

Eliphaz the Temanite and Bildad the Shuhite and Zophar the Naamathite went and did as the LORD commanded them; for the LORD had accepted Job.

And the LORD restored Job's losses when he prayed for his friends. Indeed the LORD gave Job twice as much as he had before.

➤ *Our Example*

Job is a wonderful example of an intercessor. He interceded for his family. When the rough times came and he couldn't understand the workings of God, he still held on. During this time, he wrote,

Job 13:15 Though He slay me, yet will I trust Him. Even so, I will defend my own ways before Him.

Even though his friends maligned him at the worst time of his life, he forgave them and interceded for them. Then God restored everything he had lost two-fold.

Job didn't forgive his friends so that he could receive great blessings. However, the Word says that God did restore his losses when he prayed for his friends. Great blessings come to us when we forgive those who have wronged us and intercede for them.

Abraham Interceded

When God decided to destroy Sodom and Gomorrah, He first came to Abraham.

Genesis 18:17,18 And the LORD said, "Shall I hide from Abraham what I am doing, since Abraham shall surely become a great and mighty nation, and all the nations of the earth shall be blessed in him? "

Then the Lord answered His own question.

Genesis 18:19-21 "For I have known him, in order that he may command his children and his household after him, that they keep the way of the LORD, to do righteousness and justice, that the LORD may bring to Abraham what He has spoken to him."

And the LORD said, "Because the outcry against Sodom and Gomorrah is great, and because their sin is very grievous, I will go down now and see whether they have done altogether according to the outcry against it that has come to Me; and if not, I will know."

Abraham interceded, "Lord will you spare the city for fifty righteous – for forty-five – for forty – for thirty – for twenty – for ten?"

And God agreed, "I will not destroy it for ten's sake."

Why did the Lord talk to Abraham before He destroyed the cities? In actuality, God allowed a man operating in his God-given authority to set the standard that must be reached for the cities to survive – only ten righteous people.

We see the importance of Abraham's intercession in the words of the angel.

Genesis 19:22a "Hurry, escape there. For I cannot do anything until you arrive there."

➤ *Our Example*

Years before Abraham and Lot had parted. The people of Lot had fought with the people of Abraham. Lot had been given a choice and he had taken the best for himself. Then Lot had chosen to live in Sodom and Gomorrah, the cities of sin. What was going to happen to Lot was his own fault. It was the result of his decisions. But did Abraham consider this, or did he intercede for Lot and the other people in the two cities?

Moses Interceded

Moses was on the mountain with God, when the people of Israel committed a terrible sin. They made a golden calf and fell down and worshiped it as their god.

Exodus 32:7-10 And the LORD said to Moses, "Go, get down! For your people whom you brought out of the land of Egypt have corrupted themselves. They have turned aside quickly out of the way which I commanded them. They have made themselves a molded calf, and worshiped it and sacrificed to it, and said, 'This is your god, O Israel, that brought you out of the land of Egypt!' " And the LORD said to Moses, "I have seen this people, and indeed it is a stiff-necked people! "

Notice that God no longer called them His people.

"Now therefore, let Me alone, that My wrath may burn hot against them and I may consume them. And I will make of you a great nation."

"Let Me alone, Moses, that I may destroy them!" Why did God say, "Let Me alone?"

In God's eternal purpose, He had created mankind in His image and given them dominion over this earth and everything in it. God was prevented from destroying the people by Moses. Moses as an intercessor, using his God-given authority would not "let God alone," when it came to praying for the people of Israel.

➤ *The Heart-Cry of Moses*

"Blot Me Out of Your Book"

God said he was going to destroy the children of Israel. The anguish of Moses at this time is beyond the ability of most of us to understand. What was his heart-cry? "Lord if you can't forgive them take my name out of Your book."

Exodus 32:32 'Yet now, if You will forgive their sin – but if not, I pray, blot me out of Your book which You have written."

God agreed to let the people of Israel live but then He said, "I will not go up in your midst."

Exodus 33:2a,3b "And I will send My Angel before you ... for I will not go up in your midst, lest I consume you on the way for you are a stiff-necked people."

"Leave Us Here!"

When God told Moses His presence would no longer go with them, the heart-cry of Moses was, "Then leave us here!" Moses would not go on without the presence of God.

Exodus 33:15 Then he said to Him, "If Your Presence does not go with us, do not bring us up from here."

➤ *Our Example*

What a tremendous example of intercession Moses is for us! The people had fought his leadership. They had complained at every opportunity. They had even threatened to kill him. Now, God said He was going to destroy them! From Moses' descendants, God would bring forth a new nation. That would make Moses' offspring the chosen people of God. His children and their children would be the nation of Israel. The destruction of the sinful people would confirm His ability to hear from God and lead. It would prove that in every situation, he had been right.

Instead of accepting all of this, Moses interceded for the people, and because of his intercession God allowed the people to live.

Ezekiel's Indictment

In Ezekiel's time, God sought for a man to intercede – to stand in the gap – but there was no one. Through Ezekiel, the Lord spoke a terrible indictment against the nation of Israel that is so true of our day and time that we have included all of it here.

Ezekiel 22:23-31 And the word of the LORD came to me, saying, Son of man, say to her: 'You are a land that is not cleansed or rained on in the day of indignation.'

➤ *Conspiracy of Prophets*

"The conspiracy of her prophets in her midst is like a roaring lion tearing the prey; they have devoured people; they have taken treasure and precious things; they have made many widows in her midst.

➤ *Priests Violated Law, Profaned Holy Things,*
Not Taught Holy and Unholy

"Her priests have violated My law and profaned My holy things; they have not distinguished between the holy and unholy, nor have they made known the difference between the unclean and the clean; and they have hidden their eyes from My Sabbaths, so that I am profaned among them.

➤ *Political Leaders like Wolves*

"Her princes in her midst are like wolves tearing the prey, to shed blood, to destroy people, and to get dishonest gain.

➤ *Prophets Seeing False Visions,*
Using Divination

"Her prophets plastered them with untempered mortar, seeing false visions, and divining lies for them, saying, 'Thus says the Lord God,' when the LORD had not spoken.

➤ *The People As Wicked*

"The people of the land have used oppressions, committed robbery, and mistreated the poor and needy; and they wrongfully oppress the stranger.

> *God Sought for a Man*

"So I sought for a man among them who would make a wall, and stand in the gap before Me on behalf of the land, that I should not destroy it; but I found no one. Therefore I have poured out My indignation on them; I have consumed them with the fire of My wrath; and I have recompensed their deeds on their own heads," says the Lord God.

Abraham interceded for the cities of Sodom and Gomorrah. Moses interceded for the children of Israel. But in the time of Ezekiel, God looked for one man to make intercession – to stand in the gap for his land – but there was no one. God is still looking for intercessors – for people to stand in the gap for their loved ones, for their churches, for their prophets and priests, and for their political entities.

INTERCESSION – OUR PRIVILEGE AND RESPONSIBILITY

For Spiritual Leaders

We should pray for ministers of the gospel. Since Satan can hurt so many when a leader falls, the battle is stronger against them. We should be praying regularly for our spiritual leaders.

> *To Minister Boldly*

Paul asked the believers of Ephesus to pray that he would speak boldly. We should pray that for our leaders.

Ephesians 6:19 And for me, that utterance may be given to me, that I may open my mouth boldly to make known the mystery of the gospel ...

> *For Open Doors*

He asked the believers in Colosse to pray for him to have open doors. We can still pray that today.

Colossians 4:3a Meanwhile praying also for us, that God would open to us a door for the word, to speak the mystery of Christ ...

> *That Word Will Be Glorified*
> *Deliverance from Wicked Men*

He asked the Thessalonians to pray that the word of the Lord would have free course in them and be glorified through them and that they would be delivered from unreasonable and wicked men. This is another way we are to pray for our spiritual leaders.

2 Thessalonians 3:1,2a Finally, brethren, pray for us, that the word of the Lord may have free course and be glorified, just as it is with you, And that we may be delivered from unreasonable and wicked men ...

> *To Live Honorably*

The writer of the book of Hebrews asked them to pray that they live honorably with a good conscience. This should still be our prayer today.

Hebrews 13:18 Pray for us; for we are confident that we have a good conscience, in all things desiring to live honorably.

➤ *Our Responsibility*

It was in the news about a leader in the body of Christ who had fallen into sin. People were asking us about the situation. They were disappointed – hurt. I was talking to the Lord about it. How could we help the people? God had only one reply for them and for me. "You looked up to him. You received from him, but how often did you pray for him?" It's been years since God spoke those words to me, but I have never forgotten them. We have a responsibility to pray for leaders in the body of Christ.

For Political Leaders

We are to pray for our leaders so that we can lead quiet, peaceful lives.

1 Timothy 2:1-4 Therefore I exhort first of all that supplications, prayers, intercessions, and giving of thanks be made for all men, for kings and all who are in authority, that we may lead a quiet and peaceable life in all godliness and reverence. For this is good and acceptable in the sight of God our Savior, who desires all men to be saved and to come to the knowledge of the truth.

The person who enters into a relationship of prayer for his or her nation may be able to accomplish more than those who are in the governments. God will listen to the voice of His people.

2 Chronicles 7:13,14 When I shut up heaven and there is no rain, or command the locusts to devour the land, or send pestilence among My people, if My people who are called by My name will humble themselves, and pray and seek My face, and turn from their wicked ways, then I will hear from heaven, and will forgive their sin and heal their land.

For Cities Where We Live

We are to pray for the peace of the cities where we live as this will bring us peace.

Jeremiah 29:7 And seek the peace of the city where I have caused you to be carried away captive, and pray to the LORD for it; for in its peace you will have peace.

For Those Who Persecute Us

When we can pray for the people who have caused us harm, we know we have truly forgiven them.

Matthew 5:44 "But I say to you, love your enemies, bless those who curse you, do good to those who hate you, and pray for those who spitefully use you and persecute you."

Luke 6:28 "bless those who curse you, and pray for those who spitefully use you."

For the Harvest of the Nations

Jesus told the disciples to pray for laborers and then He sent them forth into the harvest. When we begin to earnestly intercede for a need, many times God will bring the answer through us.

Luke 10:2 Then He said to them, "The harvest truly is great, but the laborers are few; therefore pray the Lord of the harvest to send out laborers into His harvest."

Psalms 2:8 Ask of Me, and I will give You The nations for Your inheritance, And the ends of the earth for Your possession.

For Israel

There is special blessing attached to prayer for God's chosen people, and for the hastening of His purposes concerning them.

Psalms 122:6,7 Pray for the peace of Jerusalem: "May they prosper who love you. Peace be within your walls, Prosperity within your palaces."

For New Converts

We should pray for those we lead to Christ.

1 Thessalonians 3:9,10 For what thanks can we render to God for you, for all the joy with which we rejoice for your sake before our God, Night and day praying exceedingly that we may see your face and perfect what is lacking in your faith?

For All Saints

We should pray for those in all parts of the world who have been saved.

Ephesians 6:18 Praying always with all prayer and supplication in the Spirit, being watchful to this end with all perseverance and supplication for all the saints.

For One Another

James encouraged us to enter into a relationship with others – to confess our sins and to pray for one another.

James 5:16 Confess your trespasses to one another, and pray for one another, that you may be healed. The effective, fervent prayer of a righteous man avails much.

For the Sick

James 5:14,15 Is anyone among you sick? Let him call for the elders of the church, and let them pray over him, anointing him with oil in the name of the Lord. And the prayer of faith will save the sick, and the Lord will raise him up. And if he has committed sins, he will be forgiven.

For the Backslider

Instead of judging or criticizing or merely pitying those who fall, we should pray for them.

Galatians 6:1,2 Brethren, if a man is overtaken in any trespass, you who are spiritual restore such a one in a spirit of gentleness, considering yourself lest you also be tempted. Bear one another's burdens, and so fulfill the law of Christ.

For Prisoners

In Hebrews we read that we are to remember the prisoners as if we were chained to them. That is more than a casual prayer.

Hebrews 13:3 Remember the prisoners as if chained with them, and those who are mistreated, since you yourselves are in the body also.

For Ourselves

It's not selfish to pray for ourselves, for as we receive blessings, we will be made a blessing to others.

1 Chronicles 4:10 And Jabez called on the God of Israel saying, "Oh, that You would bless me indeed, and enlarge my territory, that Your hand would be with me, and that You would keep me from evil, that I may not cause pain!" So God granted him what he requested.

✦ Summary – The Heart-Cry of God

God loves every man, woman and child. His desire is that all would know Him. The more we know Him and spend time with Him, the more we will understand His heart-cry for the people around us.

Intercession began with Job in the oldest book of the Bible. It continued on with Abraham, Moses and Ezekiel to name just a few. Today, Jesus is interceding for us. He is our High Priest, our Advocate, and always our best example.

The need for men and women of God to be intercessors for their families, their friends, their churches, their neighborhoods, their cities, states and countries has not changed. We are all to answer the hear-cry of God and be intercessors standing in the gap for a sinful people, releasing the power of God into their lives.

We must take time to intercede always, without ceasing, at all times, for the needs we see around us. This is one of God's greatest callings to the body of Christ today – care about those around you, intercede for them. Pray for them in the Holy Spirit and then pray as God leads in your natural language.

QUESTIONS FOR REVIEW

1. Write your definition of intercession.

2. What are the six practical steps of intercession?

3. Give three areas where the Lord is leading you to intercede. Give promises from God's Word on which you can stand.

Lesson Ten

"If You Abide in Me"

Jesus said,

John 15:7 If you abide in Me, and My words abide in you, you will ask what you desire, and it shall be done for you.

That's the wonderful promise of God concerning our prayers, but it's extremely conditional. We must abide in Him and His Word must abide in us before we can ask whatever we desire. Let's back up and consider the passage that ends with this wonderful promise

John 15:4-7 "Abide in Me, and I in you. As the branch cannot bear fruit of itself, unless it abides in the vine, neither can you, unless you abide in Me.

"I am the vine, you are the branches. He who abides in Me, and I in him, bears much fruit; for without Me you can do nothing.

"If anyone does not abide in Me, he is cast out as a branch and is withered; and they gather them and throw them into the fire, and they are burned.

"If you abide in Me, and My words abide in you, you will ask what you desire, and it shall be done for you."

How do we actually abide in Jesus? On a day-to-day basis, how is this accomplished?

ABIDING IN HIM

Moses knew God. Moses was a friend of God. There is so much to learn from the actions of Moses after the terrible sin of the Children of Israel worshiping another god – the golden calf. His attitude toward the people was not one of condemnation – but of anguish almost beyond our understanding.

Because of sin, the glory of God left the camp of Israel. God could not stay in their midst, for He would consume them. God has not changed. God cannot coexist with sin. It is contrary to His very nature.

How many have deceived themselves and others into thinking their sins are covered by grace? That no matter what they do, God will forgive them and things can go on as before. This is not true. Jesus said,

Matthew 6:24a (Amp) No one can serve two masters; for either he will hate the one and love the other, or he will stand by and be devoted to the one and despise and be against the other.

Come Outside the Camp

Because of the sin of the people, God had departed, and immediately, Moses did also. He physically moved his tent outside the camp. He didn't allow himself to become part of the sin. He didn't move because he didn't love the people. He had just put his eternal life on the line for them. He moved so that he would be free to talk with God.

Exodus 33:7a,9.11a Moses took his tent and pitched it outside the camp, far from the camp,

And it came to pass, when Moses entered the tabernacle, that the pillar of cloud descended and stood at the door of the tabernacle, and the LORD talked with Moses

So the LORD spoke to Moses face to face, as a man speaks to his friend.

Today, the glory of God has departed from many individuals, ministries, and churches because of sin. God is looking for a people who, just like Moses, will come outside the camp. He is looking for a people who will enter into close personal relationships with Him. He is looking for a people who understand Who He is, who will pray and worship Him. He is looking for those who have laid aside every hindrance to run the race.

Hebrews 12:1-4 Therefore we also, since we are surrounded by so great a cloud of witnesses, let us lay aside every weight, and the sin which so easily ensnares us, and let us run with endurance the race that is set before us, looking unto Jesus, the author and finisher of our faith, who for the joy that was set before Him endured the cross, despising the shame, and has sat down at the right hand of the throne of God.

For consider Him who endured such hostility from sinners against Himself, lest you become weary and discouraged in your souls. You have not yet resisted to bloodshed, striving against sin.

A Price to Be Paid

In the new birth we became one spirit with God.

1 Corinthians 6:17 But he who is joined to the Lord is one spirit with Him.

There is a price to be paid to be one spirit with God – to abide in Him.

The apostle Paul wrote that we were to come out from among them and be separate.

2 Corinthians 6:16,17 And what agreement has the temple of God with idols? For you are the temple of the living God. As God has said: "I will dwell in them and walk among them. I will be their God, and they shall be My people." Therefore "Come out from among them and be separate, says the Lord. Do not touch what is unclean, and I will receive you."

ABIDING IN PRAYER AND PRAISE

What is the pattern of prayer? How can we put together praying persistently and yet let our words be few? Do we stand, kneel, close our eyes? "Lord, show us how You want us to pray!"

Physical Position

Our physical position is not important. We can stand, pace, kneel, or lie prostrate on the floor. We can close our eyes or keep them open. We can sit at a table with our notebooks before us. We can enter a dark closet. We can pray out loud. We can pray silently. We can pray for hours or for minutes.

God is a God of variety! What is right for me, may not be right for you. What is right today, may not be right tomorrow. One position may be best when we are interceding, but another when we are entering into warfare.

Don't allow yourself to be "locked in a box!." If you get in a habit of praying only in your closet, wherever or whatever that may be, you will be wasting all that wonderful, useful time while you are delayed in traffic, or cleaning the house.

Our physical position is important so that we can pray with our whole heart. We cannot let our bodies rule our spirits.

Enter His Presence

We enter into prayer, the same way we enter into worship – we come into His presence with the tabernacle as our pattern. David explained the progression of coming into the presence of God.

Psalms 100:4 Enter into His gates with thanksgiving, And into His courts with praise. Be thankful to Him, and bless His name.

We can stay at the gates with thanksgiving, or go on into the courts with praise. We can go even into the Holy of Holies, into the throne room of God when we bless His name. Our petitions, our needs, our requests are still in our minds as we give Him thanksgiving, and even when we enter into praise, but when we enter the throne room of heaven all our needs are forgotten as we worship Him just for who He is.

We can come as far into God's presence as we truly desire to come – but there can be no sin in His presence.

How do we give thanksgiving? How do we give praise? How do we worship Him? As you study the next sections, let your spirit reach out to God. Learn by experiencing thanksgiving, praise and worship.

Thanksgiving

Thanksgiving is an act of giving thanks; an expression of gratitude; expressing appreciation to God for what He has done. It is an expression of joy rising from a believer's heart in appreciation for all the benefits and blessings that He has bestowed on us and other believers. Thanksgiving is a way of abiding in Him.

Thanksgiving is not taking God for granted. An unknown believer said, "When prayer is answered, forget not praise or thanksgiving. The apparently conquered enemy stands again at the door of the ungrateful heart!"

The apostle Paul wrote,
2 Corinthians 9:15 Thanks be to God for His indescribable gift!

Be thankful with David as he wrote,
Psalms 118:1 Oh, give thanks to the LORD, for He is good! Because His mercy endures forever.

Psalms 107:8 Oh, that men would give thanks to the LORD for His goodness, And for His wonderful works to the children of men!

In times of sorrow we can, by God's, grace thank Him. We can thank and praise Jesus when we are facing hard trials. The apostle Peter wrote,

1 Peter 1:6,7 In this you greatly rejoice, though now for a little while, if need be, you have been grieved by various trials, that the genuineness of your faith, being much more precious than gold that perishes, though it is tested by fire, may be found to praise, honor, and glory at the revelation of Jesus Christ.

Thanksgiving fills us with confidence and faith. It accelerates the answers to our prayers. One excellent way to spend time in thanksgiving is by reading the Psalms as your prayer to God.

Praise

Another way to abide in God is by giving Him praise. Praise is an expression of approval, commendation, or admiration. It means to extol or exalt, to magnify Him for what He has done.

David understood how important praise was because he was a praiser of God. Let's spend time now praising God with David,

Praise the LORD!
Praise the name of the LORD;
Praise Him, O you servants of the LORD! Psalms 135:1

I will bless the LORD at all times;
His praise shall continually be in my mouth. Psalms 34:1

But we will bless the LORD From this time forth and forevermore. Praise the LORD! Psalms 115:18

Oh, that men would give thanks to the LORD for His goodness,
And for His wonderful works to the children of men!
Let them exalt Him also in the congregation of the people,
And praise Him in the assembly of the elders. Psalms 107:31,32

Let heaven and earth praise Him,
The seas and everything that moves in them. Psalms 69:34

Praise the LORD!
Praise the LORD from the heavens;
Praise Him in the heights!
Praise Him, all His angels;
Praise Him, all His hosts!
Praise Him, sun and moon;
Praise Him, all you stars of light!
Praise Him, you heavens of heavens,
And you waters above the heavens!
Let them praise the name of the LORD,
For He commanded and they were created. Psalms 148:1-5

Praise the LORD!
Praise God in His sanctuary;
Praise Him in His mighty firmament!
Praise Him for His mighty acts;
Praise Him according to His excellent greatness!
Praise Him with the sound of the trumpet;
Praise Him with the lute and harp!
Praise Him with the timbrel and dance;

Praise Him with stringed instruments and flutes!
Praise Him with loud cymbals;
Praise Him with high sounding cymbals!
Let everything that has breath praise the LORD.
Praise the LORD! Psalms 150:1-6

Worship

Worship is abiding in Him in the greatest degree possible on this earth. Worship is when we come into the very presence of God. It is coming into the throne room of heaven.

The word worship means attitudes and acts of reverence to God. Worship is the bowing of the inward spirit with deep humility and reverence before Him. True worship comes from a heart filled with love and appreciation for who God is.

When we worship God, we give reverence to the worth and supreme value of God. When we worship God, we extol His attributes and honor the excellency of His name. We agree with David when he wrote,

Psalms 34:1,3 I will bless the LORD at all times; His praise shall continually be in my mouth ... Oh, magnify the LORD with me, And let us exalt His name together.

Psalms 148:13 Let them praise the name of the LORD, For His name alone is exalted; His glory is above the earth and heaven.

Psalms 8:1 O LORD, our Lord, How excellent is Your name in all the earth, You who set Your glory above the heavens!

Worship can be so sweet. We can give praises to the Lord Jesus, who by His precious blood has redeemed us to God. When we worship Him, we can join the heavenly hosts falling before Him saying,

Revelation 5:12b "Worthy is the Lamb who was slain to receive power and riches and wisdom, and strength and honor and glory and blessing!"

Even without words, we can worship God. In silence, we can meditate on God's greatness and majesty! In Job we read,

Job 37:14 "Listen to this, O Job; stand still and consider the wondrous works of God."

We can worship God through the wonders of His creation. We can marvel at the mighty mountains, the roaring waves of the sea, the hosts of the stars that decorate the night sky, so marvelous that it inspired this great song.

O Lord my God,
When I in awesome wonder,
Consider all the world Thy hands have made;
I see the stars,
I hear the roaring thunder,
Thy power throughout the universe displayed,
Then sings my soul, my Savior God to Thee;
How Great Thou art! How great Thou art!

Above sections on Thanksgiving and Worship were taken, in part, from **Meeting with God – Prayer's Deepest Meaning** *by Wilson Mamboleo.*

THE POWER OF PRAYER AND PRAISE

There are two things that we are commanded to do continuously. We are to pray without ceasing, and to praise God continuously.

Jesus said,
Luke 18:1b ... men always ought to pray ...

Luke 21:36a Watch therefore, and pray always ...

Paul wrote,
Romans 1:9b ... without ceasing I make mention of you always in my prayers ...

1 Thessalonians 2:13a For this reason we also thank God without ceasing ...

2 Timothy 1:3b ... without ceasing I remember you in my prayers night and day ...

2 Thessalonians 1:11a Therefore we also pray always for you ...

1 Thessalonians 5:16-18 Rejoice always, pray without ceasing, in everything give thanks; for this is the will of God in Christ Jesus for you.

How can we do two things simultaneously unless they be the same?

We are told that if we exercise every morning, our metabolism will speed up and, even when we are sitting at our desks, our body will go on receiving the benefits of that exercise. Prayer and praise have the same residual effect in our spirits. If we set aside a time of prayer and praise, our spirits will go on praying and praising all day.

Jehoshaphat Faces Three Armies

Jehoshaphat is a wonderful example to us of the power of prayer and praise. The kings of three nations had come against him and in the natural it was a hopeless situation. But Jehoshaphat sought the Lord and fasted and prayed.

➤ *He Prayed*

2 Chronicles 20:3,5-12 And Jehoshaphat feared, and set himself to seek the LORD, and proclaimed a fast throughout all Judah.

Then Jehoshaphat stood ... and said: "O LORD God of our fathers, are You not God in heaven, and do You not rule over all the kingdoms of the nations, and in Your hand is there not power and might, so that no one is able to withstand You?

"Are You not our God, who drove out the inhabitants of this land before Your people Israel, and gave it to the descendants of Abraham Your friend forever?

"And they dwell in it, and have built You a sanctuary in it for Your name, saying, 'If disaster comes upon us, such as the sword, judgment, pestilence, or famine, we will stand before this temple and in Your presence (for Your name is in this temple), and cry out to You in our affliction, and You will hear and save.'

"And now, here are the people of Ammon, Moab, and Mount Seir —whom You would not let Israel invade when they came out of the land of Egypt, but they turned from them and did not destroy them – here they are, rewarding us by coming to throw us out of Your possession which You have given us to inherit.

"O our God, will You not judge them? For we have no power against this great multitude that is coming against us; nor do we know what to do, but our eyes are upon You."

Notice the progression of Jehoshaphat's prayer. He started out by recognizing Who God was and what He had done. He affirmed, "Lord You gave us this land. We obeyed You when we left these inhabitants alive." He ended with the honest confession, "We don't know what to do, but our eyes are on You."

➤ *God Answered*

Then the Lord answered through Jahaziel.

2 Chronicles 20:15b-17 "Do not be afraid nor dismayed because of this great multitude, for the battle is not yours, but God's. Tomorrow go down against them. They will surely come up by the ascent of Ziz, and you will find them at the end of the brook before the Wilderness of Jeruel.

'You will not need to fight in this battle. Position yourselves, stand still and see the salvation of the LORD, who is with you, O Judah and Jerusalem!' Do not fear or be dismayed; tomorrow go out against them, for the LORD is with you."

➤ *Position Yourselves*

Jahaziel said "Position yourselves, stand still and see the salvation of the Lord." What position did he and the others take? They bowed their heads to the ground and worshiped the Lord and then they stood up and praised the Lord.

2 Chronicles 20:18,19 And Jehoshaphat bowed his head with his face to the ground, and all Judah and the inhabitants of Jerusalem bowed before the LORD, worshiping the LORD. Then the Levites of the children of the Kohathites and of the children of the Korahites stood up to praise the LORD God of Israel with voices loud and high.

➤ *Believe in the Lord*

The next morning Jehoshaphat declared the Word of the Lord. He didn't reiterate the problem again. He exhorted the people to believe, and he sent those who would sing, those who would praise, out in front of the army.

2 Chronicles 20:20,21 And they rose early in the morning and went out into the Wilderness of Tekoa; and as they went out, Jehoshaphat stood and said, "Hear me, O Judah and you inhabitants of Jerusalem: Believe in the LORD your God, and you shall be established; believe His prophets, and you shall prosper."

➤ *Sing and Praise the Lord*

And when he had consulted with the people, he appointed those who should sing to the LORD, and who should praise the beauty of holiness, as they went out before the army and were saying: "Praise the LORD, for His mercy endures forever."

When they began to sing and praise the Lord, God set ambushes against the enemy. The armies of the enemies turned on each other and destroyed themselves.

> *Enemy Defeated Themselves*

2 Chronicles 20:22,24 Now when they began to sing and to praise, the LORD set ambushes against the people of Ammon, Moab, and Mount Seir, who had come against Judah; and they were defeated.

So when Judah came to a place overlooking the wilderness, they looked toward the multitude; and there were their dead bodies, fallen on the earth. No one had escaped.

Elijah and Priests of Baal

There was an extreme manifestation of power when the fire fell from heaven and consumed Elijah's sacrifice. Remember Elijah's prayer when he was in the contest with the priests of Baal?

1 Kings 18:36b,37 "LORD God of Abraham, Isaac, and Israel, let it be known this day that You are God in Israel, and that I am Your servant, and that I have done all these things at Your word. Hear me, O LORD, hear me, that this people may know that You are the LORD God, and that You have turned their hearts back to You again."

Elijah started out by recognizing Who God was, and reminding Him that he was walking in obedience. He didn't say a word about the other priests that were against him. He didn't pray about the problem. He didn't even ask for the fire to fall and the sacrifice to be consumed. Elijah had such faith in God that he knew He was very aware of all of that. Elijah prayed the simple prayer above, and God answered.

Thanksgiving from the Fish's Belly

We have Jonah's prayer from the belly of the fish. This has to be one of the most honest, heart-felt prayers we could ever read. Jonah prayed and the fish vomited him out on the land God had sent him to. That's a demonstration of power.

Jonah 2:1-9 Then Jonah prayed to the LORD his God from the fish's belly. And he said: "I cried out to the LORD because of my affliction, and He answered me. "out of the belly of Sheol I cried, and You heard my voice.

For You cast me into the deep, into the heart of the seas, and the floods surrounded me; all Your billows and Your waves passed over me. Then I said, 'I have been cast out of Your sight; yet I will look again toward Your holy temple.' The waters encompassed me, even to my soul; the deep closed around me; weeds were wrapped around my head.

I went down to the moorings of the mountains; the earth with its bars closed behind me forever; yet You have brought up my life from the pit, O LORD, my God.

"When my soul fainted within me, I remembered the LORD; and my prayer went up to You, into Your holy temple. Those who regard worthless idols forsake their own Mercy.

But I will sacrifice to You with the voice of thanksgiving; I will pay what I have vowed. Salvation is of the LORD."

Notice that he started out, "I cried out to the Lord," but he moved to "O Lord, my God." Even in the belly of the fish, he made a prophetic statement. "I have been cast out of Your sight; yet I will look again toward Your holy temple." Also from the belly of the fish, he said, "I will sacrifice to You with the voice of thanksgiving."

David Mixed Prayer Liberally with Praise

The little unknown shepherd boy, grew up to slay the giant, and then went on to conquer nation after nation and became the king of Israel. David's life was one of praise and certainly of power. David was a man loved by God. The book of Psalms is full of praise and prayer. We can cover only a few of the examples here.

➤ *When Absalom Came Against Him*

Psalms 3:3-5 But You, O LORD, are a shield for me, My glory and the One who lifts up my head. I cried to the LORD with my voice, And He heard me from His holy hill. Selah

I lay down and slept; I awoke, for the LORD sustained me.

➤ *Hear My Call*

Psalms 4:1 Hear me when I call, O God of my righteousness! You have relieved me when I was in distress; Have mercy on me, and hear my prayer.

➤ *Give Ear to My Words*

Psalms 5:1-3 Give ear to my words, O LORD, Consider my meditation. Give heed to the voice of my cry, My King and my God, For to You I will pray. My voice You shall hear in the morning, O LORD; In the morning I will direct it to You, And I will look up.

➤ *Save Me*

Psalms 7:1 O LORD my God, in You I put my trust; Save me from all those who persecute me; And deliver me.

➤ *Let Me Not Be Ashamed*

Psalms 25:1-5 To You, O LORD, I lift up my soul. O my God, I trust in You; Let me not be ashamed; Let not my enemies triumph over me. Indeed, let no one who waits on You be ashamed; Let those be ashamed who deal treacherously without cause. Show me Your ways, O LORD; Teach me Your paths. Lead me in Your truth and teach me, For You are the God of my salvation; On You I wait all the day.

Psalms 31:1-3 In You, O LORD, I put my trust; Let me never be ashamed; Deliver me in Your righteousness. Bow down Your ear to me, Deliver me speedily; Be my rock of refuge, A fortress of defense to save me. For You are my rock and my fortress; Therefore, for Your name's sake, Lead me and guide me.

➤ *He Heard My Cry*

Psalms 40:1-3 I waited patiently for the LORD; And He inclined to me, And heard my cry. He also brought me up out of a horrible pit, Out of the miry clay, And set my feet upon a rock, And established my steps. He has put a new song in my mouth – Praise to our God; Many will see it and fear, And will trust in the LORD.

➤ *Soul Thirsts for God*

Psalms 42:1,2 As the deer pants for the water brooks, So pants my soul for You, O God. My soul thirsts for God, for the living God. When shall I come and appear before God?

➤ *Be Merciful*

Psalms 57:1-3 Be merciful to me, O God, be merciful to me! For my soul trusts in You; And in the shadow of Your wings I will make my refuge, Until these calamities have passed by. I will cry out to God Most High, To God who performs all things for me. He shall send from heaven and save me; He reproaches the one who would swallow me up. Selah God shall send forth His mercy and His truth.

➤ *Deliver Me*

Psalms 71:1-3 In You, O LORD, I put my trust; Let me never be put to shame. Deliver me in Your righteousness, and cause me to escape; Incline Your ear to me, and save me. Be my strong habitation, To which I may resort continually; You have given the commandment to save me, For You are my rock and my fortress.

DWELLING IN THE SECRET PLACE

When we abide in Christ, we become worshippers of God. When we live in the intimacy of His presence of the Holy of Holies, we are dwelling in the secret place of the Most High.

Psalms 91:1 He who dwells in the secret place of the Most High Shall abide under the shadow of the Almighty.

As we bow before His throne in a lifestyle of worship, we are abiding under the shadow of the Almighty. It is here, we delight ourselves in Him. It is here, His will becomes our desires.

Psalms 40:8 I delight to do Your will, O my God, And Your law is within my heart.

Psalms 37:4 Delight yourself also in the LORD, And He shall give you the desires of your heart.

As we abide in deep and intimate fellowship with Him, our desires are transformed from our wills to His will. Then we simply ask and He gives us the transformed desires of our heart.

What did Jesus say?

John 15:7 If you abide in Me, and My words abide in you, you will ask what you desire, and it shall be done for you.

✦ Summary – "If You Abide in Me"

Oh, men and women of God, what a wonderful privilege is ours – what an awesome responsibility. Let's come outside the camp. Let's move more and more into the presence of God. Let's learn to give thanksgiving to Him morning, noon and night. Let's learn to praise Him without ceasing. Let's learn to worship at His feet so that we can be changed more and more into His likeness. Let's position ourselves for victory! Let's pray His will into existence on our earth. Let's bring heaven to earth!

QUESTIONS FOR REVIEW

1. What is the pattern for entering into prayer?

2 In 2 Chronicles 20:18, God told Jehoshaphat to position himself for victory. What did Jehoshaphat do?

3. Why do you think God told believers to both pray and praise without ceasing?

4. Write your own definition of prayer.